Alfred W. Tatum

FEARLESS**VOICES**

Engaging a New Generation of African American Adolescent Male Writers

Foreword by Marcelle Haddix

SCHOLASTIC

New York • Toronto • London • Auckland • Sydney
Mexico City • New Delhi • Hong Kong • Buenos Aires

Dedication

This book is dedicated to the Brother Authors who wrote and continue to write
to preserve this nation one word at a time.

Credits: **page 39:** Photo of Edmund Perry: Marilynn K. Yee/The New York Times/Redux. **page 159:** Olaudah Equiano: Project Gutenberg; Absalom Jones: The Granger Collection; James Forten: The Granger Collection. **page 160:** Rev. Peter Williams: Manuscripts, Archives and Rare Books Division, Schomburg Center for Research in Black Culture, The New York Public Library, Astor, Lenox and Tilden Foundations; Samuel Cornish: The Granger Collection; Rev. Theodore S. Wright: Courtesy of the Randolph Linsly Simpson African-American Collection, Beinecke Rare Book & Manuscript Library, Yale University. John Russwurm: Courtesy the Bowdoin College Library, Brunswick, Maine; William Whipper: From William Still's book "The Underground Railroad"/Lancaster Historical Society. **page 161:** David Ruggles: Levellers Press; Robert Purvis: Boston Public Library, Print Department; Martin Delaney: Library of Congress, Prints & Photographs Division; Henry Highland Garnet: The Granger Collection; James McCune Smith: The Granger Collection; William Wells Brown: Project Gutenberg. **page 162:** William C. Nell: www.theliberatorfiles.com; Samuel Ringgold Ward: From the book: *Autobiography of a Fugitive Negro: His Anti-Slavery Labours in the United States, Canada, & England*; Frederick Douglass: Bettmann/Corbis; Alexander Crummell: General Research and Reference Division, Schomburg Center for Research in Black Culture, The New York Public Library, Astor, Lenox and Tilden Foundations; Booker T. Washington: Library of Congress Prints & Photographs; Paul Laurence Dunbar: Ohio Historical Society, Library of Congress. **page 163:** Charles Chesnutt: Cleveland Public Library Digital Gallery; W.E.B. Du Bois: Library of Congress Prints & Photographs Online Catalog; Alain Locke: The Granger Collection; James W. Johnson: The Granger Collection; Claude McKay: Corbis; Charles S. Johnson: Library of Congress Prints and Photographs Division. **page 164:** Jean Toomer: Bettmann/Corbis; Rudolph Fisher: The Granger Collection; Sterling Brown: Scurlock Studio Records, Archives Center, NMAH, Smithsonian Institution; Arna Bontemps: Library of Congress Prints & Photographs; Langston Hughes: Courtesy of the Yale Collection of American Literature, Beinecke Rare Book and Manuscript Library; Countee Cullen: Bettmann/Corbis. **page 165:** Amiri Baraka: Anthony Barboza/Getty Images; Elridge Cleaver: Marion S. Trikosko/U.S. News & World Report Magazine Collection/Library of Congress; James Baldwin: Miami Dade County Archives; Robert Hayden: Oscar White/Pach Brothers/Corbis; Ralph Ellison: Courtesy of the National Archives; Richard Wright: Van Vechten Collection/Library of Congress Prints & Photographs Online Catalog. **page 166:** Walter Dean Myers: Courtesy of Walter Dean Myers; John Edgar Wideman: Geoffrey A. Landis; Don Lee/Haki Madhubuti: Third World Press; Ellis Cose: Greg Barrett; Walter Mosley: David Shankbone. **page 167:** Nathan McCall: Courtesy of Nathan McCall; Percival Everett: Charly Triballeau/Getty Images; Michael Eric Dyson: Bennett Raglin/Getty Images; John McWhorter: Courtesy Manhattan Institute for Policy Research; Kevin Powell: Courtesy of Michael Scott Jones; Aaron McGruder: Lucy Nicholson/AP Photo.

Cover Designer: Brian LaRossa
Editor: Lois Bridges
Copy/Production Editor: Danny Miller
Interior Designer: Sarah Morrow

Copyright © 2013 by Alfred W. Tatum
All rights reserved. Published by Scholastic Inc.
Printed in the U.S.A.
ISBN: 978-0-545-43929-9

2   3   4   5   6   7   8   9   10   23   18   17   16   15   14   13

CONTENTS

Key Point: There is a long-storied tradition of African American male writers unknown to this generation of potential writers.

Key Point: Dehumanization is overcome by reminding oneself and others of the right to be whole and fully present in the world.

Key Point: To write is to grow intellectually. Intellect is a tool of protection; therefore, writing is a tool of protection.

Key Point: Loving others imbues our leadership with hope and possibility and builds our capacity to help.

Key Point: Writing carries a unique burden for the writer, his contemporaries, and future generations, particularly writing that deals with socially and politically explosive phenomena such as race and Blackness in the United States. To write about such issues for future generations requires thoughtful analysis, courage, and a bit of luck.

Key Point: To write is to become familiar with your light and darkness and everything in between. It becomes the gray matter of your existence. Reading puts you in contact with others. Writing puts you in contact with yourself.

Appendix

ACKNOWLEDGMENTS

It seems as though every movement has a strong woman who figures prominently. Karen Proctor is that strong figure for what I hope will become a writer's movement for African American males and other students across the nation for years to come. The idea for the African American Adolescent Male Summer Literacy Institute was birthed from an innocent lunch conversation in which I was asked, "What would you like to do to take your work into the community?" I responded, "I want to nurture the next generation of writers. This can be the first generation of African American males without their voices on record." I am grateful that Karen Proctor asked the question and provided support for our first Institute, held in the summer of 2008. Her steady support and sturdy vision have given rise to a new generation of writers. During that first summer, she visited the University of Illinois at Chicago to witness young males writing in a hot room amid blowing fans. Yet, the young African American writers who were using their pens to shout and whisper refused to be deterred by the physical environment. The mental landscapes that they were constructing surpassed all else.

I would also like to thank Scholastic for its ongoing support of the research that led to this text and the national writing program, *ID: Voice, Vision, and Identity*. Scholastic's commitment to the education of young folks in the United States and beyond is palpable. I was fortunate to work with a team of leaders who pushed my thinking as they allowed me to push theirs. Scholastic also had the brilliant insight to match me with an editor with an insightful eye and human touch, Lois Bridges. Her support and encouragement during the writing of this text were extraordinary. Lois challenged me to write clearly and honestly. This book is a hopeful text because of her.

I also want to acknowledge the support provided by several graduate students at the University of Illinois at Chicago who allowed me to simply write as they protected the sanctity of the writing space. I was fortunate to work with Dr. Valerie Jones, Darius Presley, Shary Rubin, and Gholdy Muhammad. They made the Institute a success and can take a measure of credit for the writings of the young males found within these pages.

Finally, I want to thank the young Brother Authors and their parents who trusted me during the Institutes and taught me during our times together. I am forever changed. In the years ahead, I am looking forward to revisiting and rereading the words of the Brother Authors and experiencing the exhilaration, promise, and idealism all over again. *Long live the Brother Authors!*

FOREWORD

by Marcelle Haddix

"They're writing underground. When you see them walking down the halls, you would never know that they are writers"—with their baggy jeans, black hoodies, and Jordans, their afros, dreadlocks, and high top fades. A student shared with me how black male students in his school were stereotyped because of their physical appearance and fashion choices and not seen as or believed to be writers. Implicit in his declaration was the feeling that many had bought into the hype that African American adolescent males don't and can't write. The existence of this underground writing collective, for me, spoke to a broader issue—that there is a need to cultivate safe, welcoming public spaces for African American adolescent males to reclaim their writer identities.

This need is imminent, especially given that at every turn, there are mainstream messages and images that represent African American males as criminal, violent, self-destructive, and dying. In education, we are inundated with reports that African American males are failing socially and academically. We are overwhelmed with research and practice that constructs African American males as underachieving, disengaged, disinterested, and resistant to teaching and learning. There is a manufactured crisis that locates African American males as menaces to society. A dominant narrative that suggests that being black and male is antithetical and oppositional to being literate and intellectual. The present and future lives of African American adolescent males depend on the disrupting and challenging of that narrative by their own fearless voices.

This most recent undertaking of Alfred Tatum's is a testament to that. He takes us into the world of young African American men—past, present, and future—who are writing their lives. Highlighting the writing practices of Brother Authors in his summer institutes, Tatum reintroduces us to young men who seek spaces that encourage writing for real audiences and for real purposes; that value writing that is personal and political; and that free the Brother Authors to express themselves in their own voices and from their perspectives. In *Fearless Voices*, Tatum offers a teaching and curricular framework for centering the writing practices of African American adolescent males who write to define themselves, to nurture their resilience, to engage with others past and present, and to build capacity for future generations of African American male writers. Throughout the book, Alfred Tatum shares examples from the young Brother Authors as well as his own writings in the spirit of cultivating this writing collective. His reintroduction and reimagining of African American adolescent male writers expands our definitions of what counts as writing and of who can be a writer.

So, *don't believe the hype*. African American males are using their pens and journals, their laptops, cell phones and mobile devices, their spray cans and microphones to fearlessly rewrite, redefine, and reclaim who they are. In *Fearless Voices*, we are welcomed into a space that acknowledges, honors, and builds upon these rhetorical traditions created and sustained by African American males.

Adolescents . . . benefit from consistent, compelling literacy instruction—images, data/numbers/texts, new information— namely, high-quality instruction and high-quality texts, aimed at helping them wrestle with issues and circumstances related to their academic, personal, and social identities, and to the identities of others.

—Alfred W. Tatum

PART 1

WRITING THEIR LIVES

In 1829, when David Ruggles was 19 years old, it is likely he read David Walker's pamphlet, *An Appeal to the Colored Citizens of the World* that "hit American society like a bomb" (Hodges, 2010, p. 40). Ruggles was part of a youthful cohort of frustrated, intelligent, ambitious, and well-educated activists. He was a fiery, pioneering journalist who wrote hundreds of letters to abolitionist newspapers, authored and published five pamphlets, and edited the first African American magazine, the *Mirror of Liberty*, during a time period when the Negro male was viewed as too degraded to be a citizen. He opened the first Black bookstore and reading room in New York City and published his own pamphlet in 1834. His achievements show the autonomy African American males found in the world of print. David Ruggles, who died at the age of 39, would have been safer if he'd kept silent. Yet, he insisted on writing to improve the conditions of his people. Young Ruggles wrote, "The pleas of crying soft and sparing never answered the purpose of a reform, and never will" (Hodges, 2010, p. 43).

> **KEY POINT**
>
> There is a long-storied tradition of African American male writers unknown to this generation of potential writers.
>
> —Alfred W. Tatum

Many of the earlier African American male writers lived in the Northern part of the United States, and wrote to dismantle the twin evils of slavery and inequality. Their writings challenged token abolitionism. In 1834, when Ruggles was 24, it is believed that white rioters set dogs against African American students at the African Free School in New York. The rioters were fueled by the incendiary articles in abolitionist newspapers, which were said to have "inflamed the public mind" (Hodges, 2010, p. 64). Writing for African American males often meant the risk of personal assault, particularly for African American males who traveled below the Mason-Dixon Line. Like Ruggles, many of these writers were fearless.

African American males have turned to writing for more than two centuries to make sense of their present conditions and shape possibilities (Mullane, 1993). They wrote to provide useful perspectives on current events and historical orientations that informed their lives. African American males embraced writing as a pipeline for personal engagement and transformation at a time when it was dangerous to write both for Blacks and Whites who focused on issues of freedom and equality. Writing could easily make a white man a martyr. This was the case with Elijah Lovejoy who penned antislavery views in St. Louis, Missouri, in the mid-1800s. He later moved to Alton, Illinois, where he was shot and killed on a November night in 1837 by a mob of whites who were determined to silence his voice. Imagine the courage it took for an African American male to write to challenge the racial status quo.

Although their ability to write for change was called into question, many African American males embraced literary and cultural strivings during the late 1800s and early 1900s as a form of self-improvement. Writing became an act of self-assertion, a duty, and a way to establish equal standing and a right to a literary public space. It was in this tradition several years ago that I began the African American Adolescent Male Summer Literacy Institute (AAAMSLI) at the University of Illinois at Chicago. The Institute was premised on the beliefs that African American male adolescents could write in order to:

- Shatter blockades to their human development
- Become smarter
- Help others understand their experiences across multiple in-school and out-of-school contexts
- Use their voices to shape a richer narrative about what it means to be young, African American, and male in the United States
- Provide insight into their multi-textured realities
- Become this generation's cultural bearers as they write to add a modern-day signature that builds upon a rich historical tradition among African American males

Inundated with news accounts of violence, I viewed the pens of young African American males as one pathway to physical and psychological survival. Confronting the stark reality many of them face in rural, suburban, and urban schools in some of the nation's most economically depressed areas and where high numbers of African American youth and adults die as a result of gun violence (e.g., Chicago, Detroit, Los Angeles), I questioned whether engaging them with writing was imbued with false promises or real possibilities. I also questioned whether teachers would be allowed to carve out a space for writing in schools throughout the nation in which so much attention is focused on improving students' ability to comprehend narrative and expository texts. After working with these young males and providing them with opportunities to read and write meaningful texts that allowed them to afford themselves deference as they engaged both intellectually and emotionally, I became convinced that writing is not only an appropriate pathway of human development, but an essential pathway. The young males I wrote with became "salvaged by their own cylinders." This is reflected in the writing by a 15-year-old who wrote the following poem.

Salvaged from a Cylinder

by Preston Davis

Who writes with his own pen?
I regret to say seldom
For men write with the pen of their ancestors
The pen of their friends
The pen of borrowed ideas
The pen of recreated ideas
Who writes with his own pen?
Some write in pencil afraid that their thoughts could be a mistake.
When indeed a mistake is made here, for the grand mistake is to believe one's
      inner workings as flaw.
Would you not write because you wanted to do so?
Or would you write to please others, to spin off of their ideals to impress whoever
      is reading or listening.
My writing is tattooed; it is etched into my skin, into my being
From hours of pain, moments of relief and days of happiness.
I write with my own pen because it's awkward to hold someone else's.
I write with my own pen because I have the most interesting things to say.
I write with my own pen because their ink is black and mine is dark grey.
And I write with my own pen because to write with anyone else's would be a
      foolish endeavor.
And you can read my story; it's written all over my face.

I needed the stories written all over their faces that this young author mentions in the final line of the poem. African American male adolescents were being "caricatured" in the national imagination without sharing their voices in traditional print forms such as essays, poems, short stories, or children's literature. Instead, they were being cast by the barrage of violence reported in newspaper accounts and the parading of statistics in policy reports, professional journals, and the popular press highlighting their school-related failures. The violent outgrowth in many large urban areas coupled with their eerie silence sickened me. I became concerned that this would be a generation of young males without their voices on record. I wanted African American adolescent males to write to stop the violence affecting their communities or at least write to help us understand their existence within their cultural and community milieu.

I have been asked on multiple occasions to make sense of the hope of literacy as an antidote to violence during speaking engagements and through my own writing. On many occasions while writing this book in my home office, my thoughts were interrupted as I scanned breaking news alerts in my local newspaper to read about the death of another young African American male. I would often sit quietly for extended periods of time in search of solutions. It became clear that some focused action and direct participation involving African American male adolescents was required. I wrote a note to myself that read, "A murder has never been committed with a pen in the right hand and the mind of the revolution." These 19 words propelled me to action. I began to contemplate how I could make sense of these young men's experiences, tap into their voices, and engage them to focus on multigenerational success. The focus on writing emerged.

A focus on writing and African American male adolescents represents a shift in my work. For years, I focused on teaching reading to these young males. As a reading teacher, I was working to give them access to texts residing outside of their lives. I viewed texts as "soft mentors" written by authors other than themselves. Increasingly, however, I needed to access the texts residing inside of them. The focus on writing led me to excavate historical fiction and nonfiction to find direction for establishing a frame for writing for today's young males. I hit the library stacks to read the writings of African American males from the past three hundred years, finding archives of a long-storied tradition of African American male writers. I wanted to avoid literacy missteps that would contribute to African American male adolescents becoming metaphorically weak and wounded by another failed approach to engage them with print. I became concerned that efforts to engage African American male adolescents with writing is often undermined by ahistorical approaches such as giving young males writing prompts in preparation for state assessments. Literacy instruction that does not acknowledge the scale and scope on the three occurring phenomena—academic disengagement, community violence, and high dropout and failure rates—will ultimately fall short and be rejected by many African American male adolescents who will not view reading or writing as legitimate tools for their own development and protection.

Four platforms for writings among African American males appeared during my excavation of texts. They are: *defining self, nurturing resilience, engaging others,* and *building capacity.* I will discuss each in greater detail throughout this book. In the summer of 2007, having identified these platforms, I decided to host five-week Summer Literacy Institutes with African American male adolescents in a university setting to determine if the platforms would lead to their engagement as writers.

During the first year, I recruited young African American males who resided in or attended schools in economically depressed communities in Chicago. The first year's participants had a wide range of writing abilities and varying dispositions toward writing that included a love affair with writing, a fear of writing, and an expressed dislike. I opened the second, third, and fourth years of the Institutes to young African American males from urban and suburban communities. During the second, third, fourth, and fifth years, most of the young males were encouraged by some adult (e.g., parent, teacher, counselor, probation officer, community activist) to apply for the Institute because the adults believed the males were having culturally and academically isolating experiences in their schools. I will take you into the writings of these young males throughout this book to shed more light on their experiences.

Over a five-year period working with 65 young males ranging in age from 11 to 17 years old, I witnessed and helped them pen more than 500 pieces. They became intellectually, culturally, socially, and emotionally invested in writing to shape their lives. Several of them recognized the urgency of their writings as they became outraged and horrified by the possible political and economic dissolution of African American males in the United States. An eighth-grade male captures this concern using the gun as a metaphor (see poem at right).

bang bang
you hear guns go off
more bodies drop
but
the clock still
goes
tick tock

His use of "tick tock" invokes a sense of time. How long will African American males continue to matter? Some will argue that they no longer matter. The United States has witnessed the partial economic collapse and social malaise in American cities such as East St. Louis, Illinois, and Detroit, Michigan (Tate, 2008). These urban landscapes, not unlike many others, have become negatively impacted by decimated economic bases and associated social unrest. Has time run out on these cities and similar communities, or will they recover the vitality they once had? It is not my intent to single out these two metropolitan areas, but to suggest that any community will be plagued by social chaos and economic turmoil wherever people suffer from educational, economic, and political weakness. These facts require a *rewriting* by African American males whose lives are centered in much of the turmoil.

My efforts during the Writing Institutes were to move five groups of African American male adolescents in the right direction. I wanted them to use their pens to change course. They were charged to seek power and promise in their own words. Inspired by the four platforms—defining self, nurturing resilience, engaging others, and building capacity—the young males recited the following Preamble at the beginning of each writing session:

We, the Brother Authors, will seek to use language to define who we are, become and nurture resilient beings, write for the benefit of others and ourselves, and use language prudently and unapologetically to mark our times and mark our lives. This, we agree to, with a steadfast commitment to the ideals of justice, compassion, and a better humanity for all. To this end, we write!

These young African American males were asked to wrestle with their existence as a group, to examine if their existence as a group was in jeopardy because of the range of maladaptive behaviors that affected them. They were given the space to scribble to recreate themselves and mold their futures, not only for themselves, but to reclaim promise for their posterity. I wrote the poem below to capture this reclamation.

You think I am crazy

Watch how crazy I am

As a scribble

To recreate myself

To remove your audacious lies

To shut you up

So I can hear my God

Who created me in His image

To you poor painters and funky
    mendacious sketchers

Your images are based on false
    theories

And cultural erasure

Get out the way

And watch me work

Watch me write

Watch me reclaim my gravitas

Reclaim my youth that you frequently
    attack

Watch me live again

For me and my sons to come

—Alfred W. Tatum

As these young African American males embraced writing, they continued to wrestle with the audience and their roles as writers. Who cared about their writing was difficult to reconcile, particularly in light of their long existence in the United States and their relatively poor position in the country's racial hierarchy. We often debated if there was a difference between a "writer" and a "Black writer." Their views were mixed. Therefore, we agreed to place the focus on the merits of their writing. Either it was good writing or not. Our litmus test was straightforward. Is this writing worth a dime or a dollar? Did the writer take care with his messages and his words? Is this writing worth reading outside of the Institute? Is there evidence that the author knows the conventions and mechanics of writing? Is the writing a "back-pocket-piece" that other people would want to read over and over again or pass on to others?

During each Institute, the young males experienced a fundamental shift in their thinking that writing was strictly for other people in favor of writing for oneself. The young males teetered between the promises of writing amid social perils. I recall a young male who joined me during the first Institute after some run-ins with the law, shouting out, "Man we are sitting here writing like this is really going to change something." Another young male in year three asked, "Why are we writing anyway? What is this going to change?" They questioned the power of writing early on in both Institutes. I responded, not orally but in writing, to both of their questions. For the first questioner, I wrote a short story that I shared the following day. For the second questioner, I penned a poem. For you, as the reader of this text, I provide a joint response to the questioners below. It is the ghost that haunts me as I think about the role of writing in the lives of many young African American males who have become despondent because of life circumstances or have lost confidence in themselves as accomplished readers and writers (see poem below).

The poem suggests options—stabbing at death as a violent reaction or a form of surrender or writing a new beginning as a form of resistance and self-empowerment. The pages that follow represent the latter.

My work with 65 African American males across five summers began as a cultural pursuit, a deeply African American people-centered approach aimed at improving the lot of a cultural and gendered group in which I have full membership. I waited eagerly each summer as they appeared for the first time in gym shoes, ties, shorts, and with sweaty palms. I had chatted with parents, teachers, and community workers about their aspirations for these young boys. I read the writing samples the young males submitted as part of the application process. I responded to e-mails and telephone calls with words of care and encouragement—all with the hope of engaging a new generation of writers.

> Defeat stands at my door
> Beating with the fury of a warrior
> Hell bent on snatching my last breath
> I stand with a pen in my hand
> My only instrument of resistance
> Do I stab at death with it?
> Or, do I write a new beginning?
>
> —Alfred W. Tatum

In the following chapters, I share the framing of the Institutes, the instructional practices that led to hundreds of pieces over a span of 63 days, the instructional context, and more importantly, the writing. Each chapter begins with a key point that frames the chapter and ends with critical questions for consideration. This text is for those who have yet to find the power of the pen and the prominent role it can play in the lives of Black boys. It is also for those who recognize the power of the same but who need a little push in places that have become resistant to writing because of other demands that have squeezed writing out or limited writing instruction to process, mechanics, and grammar. Ultimately, it is for all who are ready to embrace a new national imagination for Black boys and how they can be directly involved in shaping that imagination. The lives they write or rewrite may be the very lives that save us all.

Awareness of being Black is the most powerful and the most fertile single inspiration for Black writers in America. It is ironic that Blackness, for so long regarded as a handicap socially and culturally, should also be an artistic strength . . . . All writers arrive at a reconciliation of a sense of tradition and a sense of difference. For nearly all Black writers in America that sense of difference was the recognition of Blackness. For nearly all, but not all. Being Black was less important for Charles Chesnutt than it was for James Baldwin. But for most, Blackness was the spur, the barb, or the shirt of pain that moved the artist to achieve distinction.

—Davis and Walden, 1970, p. 13-14

CHAPTER 1

ON DEFINING SELF

In this chapter, I describe one of the platforms of African American male writers—*defining self*. Defining self involves finding the language to put your voice on record without apology and without waiting for others to define you. For African American males, this has meant wrestling with their "Blackness" in America's context. The complexity of self-definition has intensified as African American male writers continue to define their "Blackness" in relationship to maleness, to sexual orientation, to mixed-racial identity, and other associated hybrids of being Black and something else or just something else when the idea of being Black is denied by the individual. It is not uncommon to hear some African American males utter, "I am not Black, I am an American." However, it is often "Blackness" that places today's African American male youth under surveillance for failure or behavioral misconduct inside and outside of schools. I agree with Thomas Jefferson who wrote the following In *Notes on the State of Virginia* in 1781, "The phenomenon of the intersection of Blackness and maleness in the United States put many young males under surveillance as they enter social, political, and education contexts in the United States."

> **KEY POINT**
>
> Dehumanization is overcome by reminding oneself and others of the right to be whole and fully present in the world.
>
> —Alfred W. Tatum

I recall having to make sense of my racialized identity for the first time as an eleven-year-old boy. Chicago's Bridgeport neighborhood was one of the most, if not *the* most, racist neighborhoods in the city. African Americans were aware that they should not walk the streets of Bridgeport at night. This was considered a clear act of provocation to the neighborhood residents, who often attacked African Americans. I am all too familiar with this reality. The day before my older brother was scheduled to take his eighth-grade graduation photos, his eye was blackened (by a racist thug/neighborhood bully) as he was placing groceries in my aunt's car. My aunt often shopped in one of Bridgeport's grocery stores after dark, refusing to be barred from a neighborhood within a five-mile radius of where she lived. This was in 1980.

Within one month of the physical assault on my older brother, I entered the Bridgeport neighborhood for the first time to compete in my school district's oratorical and academic competition. As a sixth-grade student, I was a member of a team that competed in an Academic Olympics competition. District 11, a part of the Chicago Public Schools, included schools in highly segregated Black and White neighborhoods. Our all-African American school team won the overall competition, defeating the perennial winners that included magnet schools with predominantly white student populations. Proud of my team's victory, my mother decided to purchase a hot dog and fountain soda for me at a corner store near one of the bus stops in Bridgeport. We believed we were protected by the afternoon's sun. To my dismay, the white clerk spit in the fountain soda, turning her back to us in an attempt to hide her transgression. The trophy I held proudly lost its luster. I became "Black" in that moment because I was now a part of something deeply rooted and storied. The racist tentacles that I had only read or heard about reached me. I was forced to make sense of my own experience. Reflecting on the incident more than 30 years later, I wrote a poem to recapture the experience (see right).

The bitterness of the moment is gone, but I will not forget the experience. It was pivotal in my human development. I began to interpret the world through colored filters. Shortly after this incident, I spotted Dick Gregory's novel *Nigger* (1964) on a bookshelf in my neighborhood library, and I gravitated toward the text. I am not sure if the title would have had the same pull before the incident, but now I had been "niggerized"—injured by "the strange career of a troublesome word" (Kennedy, 2003). I was hoping Dick Gregory's book would help me make sense of my own experience. Additionally, I was struck by the words *over one million copies sold* that graced the book cover. I wondered why a million people had bought this book. His text became the first

SPIT

by Alfred W. Tatum

How dare you approach this counter!
And ask for a drink
Your thirst is weak
Compared to my hatred for your kind
Did you read the manual?
Scribbled with historical renderings
Your mother should have known better
Did she expect me to see you as a child?
Here's a little reminder for you both
I'll place it in your cup
Drink up

of my textual lineage (Tatum, 2009). In 1964, Dick Gregory had the presence of mind to co-opt the word "nigger" as he used this hate-laced term as the title of his book. He understood the importance of seizing the power to define oneself in an environment that found his very presence reprehensible. The dedication of his book is brilliant. It reads, "Dear Momma—Wherever you are, if ever you hear the word "nigger" again, remember they are advertising my book."

It is quite possible the white store clerk was acting under a prevailing philosophy. In *Masterpieces of Negro Elegance 1818–1913* (Dunbar, 2000), which contains 51 speeches by African American men and women is a reprint of "Education for Manhood" by Kelly Miller, who wrote:

> *The traditional relation of the American Negro to the society of which he forms a part is too well known to need extensive treatment in this collection. The African slave was introduced into this country as a pure animal instrumentality to perform the rougher work under the dominion of his white lord and master. There was not the remotest thought of his human personality . . . . The white race, in its arrogant conceit, constituted the personalities and the Negro the instrumentalities. Man may be defined as a distinction-making animal. He is ever prone to set up barriers between members of his own species and to deny one part of God's human creatures the inalienable birthright vouchsafed to all alike. But the process was entirely logical and consistent with the prevailing philosophy. (p. 319)*

African American males, stirred by the doctrine "all men are created equal," wrote to challenge the prevailing philosophy that was enforced legally from the mid to late 1600s to the late 1960s. Many of their writings focused on their wretched condition with the goal of moving beyond it. The predominant theme of identity, that is defining oneself, existed and continues to exist. African American male writers continue to wrestle with two questions related to identity in their writings: 1) Who am I? and 2) What does it mean to be a Black male in America?

Although the definitions of "being Black" have changed over the years, the phrases "Black Male in America" and "On Being Black" appear in titles of a wide range of texts, both fiction and nonfiction. Examples include Nathan McCall's (1994) *Makes Me Wanna Holler: A Young Black Man in America* and Ellis Cose's (2002) *The Envy of the World: On Being a Black Man in America*. In 1970, an edited volume entitled *On Being Black, Writings by Afro-Americans from Frederick Douglass to the Present* was compiled and edited by two writers, who included the works of James Baldwin, Arna Bontemps, Charles Chesnutt, Eldridge Cleaver, W. E. B Du Bois, Ralph Ellison, Langston Hughes, LeRoi Jones, Claude McKay, and Richard Wright, all of whom have expressed different, often conflicting definitions of Blackness. Yet, defining self was a signature of these writers.

Several authors wrote about their definition of Blackness in relation to how others attempted to define them. For example, Gordon Parks in *Born Black* (1970) wrote the following paragraph under the chapter heading "What I want, what I am, what you force me to be is what you are":

For I am you, staring back from a mirror of poverty and despair, of revolt and freedom. Look at me and know that to destroy me is to destroy yourself . . . We are not so far apart as it might seem. There is something about both of us that goes deeper than blood or Black or White. It is our common search for a better life, a better world . . . . I too am America. America is me. It gave me the only life I know—so I must share in its survival. There is yet a chance for us to live in peace beneath these restless skies. (p. 7)

Gordon Parks' words are striking, but so are the words of an African American male adolescent who I spoke with in November 2011 when I visited the English classroom of a group of youth locked up in the Cook County Juvenile Detention Center in Chicago. We were discussing writing and the role it could play in their lives because the principal had recently purchased a writing program, *ID: vision: voice: identity*, based on my work and published by Scholastic. When exiting, the young male shared with me the full text he had written:

> Who am I?
>
> I am a lost soul.

The profundity of his words suggests that we need education that enriches students with words, nurtures their ability to compose for their own benefit and for the society at large, and challenges literacy practices that leave our students empty of words. The final two pages of Richard Wright's *Black Boy* (1945) should be studied by young writers. He writes about the power of having words to hurl at one's darkness. He wrote:

I sat alone in my room, watching the sun sink slowly in the chill May sky. I was restless. I rose to get my hat; I wanted to visit some friends and tell them what I felt, to talk. Then I sat down. Why do that? My problem was here, with me, here in this room, and I would solve it alone here or not at all. Yet, I did not want to face it; it frightened me. I rose again and went out into the streets. Halfway down the block I stopped, undecided. Go back . . . I returned to my room and sat again, determined to look squarely at my life.

Well, what had I got out of living in this city? What had I got out of living in the South? What had I got out of living in America? I paced the floor, knowing that all I possessed were words and dim knowledge and that my country had shown me no examples of how to live a human life. All my life I had been full of a hunger for a new way to live . . .

I picked up a pencil and held it over a sheet of white paper, but my feelings stood in the way of my words. Well, I would wait, day and night, until I knew what to say. Humbly now, with no vaulting dream of achieving a vast unity, I wanted to try to build a bridge of words between me and that world outside, that world which was so distant and elusive that it seemed unreal.

I would hurl words into this darkness and wait for an echo, and if an echo sounded, no matter how faintly, I would send other words to tell, to march, to fight, to create a sense of hunger for life gnaws in us all, to keep alive in our hearts a sense of the inexpressibly human. (pp. 383–384)

As the leader of the Writing Institutes, I gave African American male adolescents permission to explore language, to express themselves eloquently, to build a bridge, and to hurl words. How I engaged them to write to define "self" will be discussed in the remainder of this chapter.

Hurling Words Into Darkness: The Application Process

Identifying the defining-self platform that existed in the writings of African American males, I decided to provide applicants the opportunity to write from a uniquely African American male perspective. As part of the application process the young men had the option to:

- Write a poem or short story that captured a contemporary African American male experience.

- Accept or defy the use of the word *monster* as an accurate descriptor of young African American males.

- Identify and address one myth about African American males.

- Submit a writing sample of their choice.

The writings about self began to pour in. Out of the more than 300 applications I received over the past four years, I was particularly punched in the heart by the last five words of the following piece.

> When I die I wanna go to hell, 'cause imma piece of sh** it ain't hard to tell . . . I ain't gettin sh** this Christmas. I hate life. Who said I wanted to be born? I don't care who don't cry at my funeral and I don't care who mourns. Why is it I'm always messin' up in stupid situations? Why do I need to find an occupation? I don't care who loves me, which nobody does. They don't even know the definition of love. Can't talk to God cuz he either acts like he's not there or he just doesn't wanna hear my prayer. This sh** makes me mad that's why I start to write . . . . If I lost my life would anybody care? My mom probably will say, "Finally, that piece of sh** is out my hair." Besides I don't believe in gettin saved. I probably won't go nowhere once I'm in my grave . . . I feel like I wanna die, but I probably won't later. I wonder what would my dad do if he saw it in the paper? I'm overlappin my life like an extra layer. Oh, and I hope dat God actually heard dat prayer; I hope nobody feels bad for me and I forgive all da people who was mad at me. I'm always getting hit wit quotes from the bible, do you wanna kill me? Do you wanna kill me? I'm speakin to my rifle. Do you wanna kill me? I'm speakin to my rifle. Hell, if you don't, either way, **I'm gonna do the suicidal.**

This piece was submitted by this young male's mother who called me early one morning and spoke frantically about what her son had written. We spoke for more than an hour as I sat at the International House of Pancakes, my breakfast growing cold. She peppered me with questions: "Is this the type of application you accept? How do you plan to write with my son? Do you think he will be a perfect fit for the other young males you plan to accept? Do you have recommendations for other summer programs if you do not accept him?"

As I answered the questions, I recall sharing with the mother that I would seriously consider accepting her son for the Institute. In my heart, I already knew that he would be selected to participate. This was the type of writing that demanded a response.

Similar to Richard Wright's piece, the 14-year-old applicant embedded questions in his writing that he then responded to. This is a hallmark of writing to define self that can be used as a teaching tool. I offer comparisons in the charts below.

Richard Wright	14-year-old Applicant
• What had I got out of living in this city? • What had I got out of living in the South? • What had I got out of living in America?	• Why is it I'm always messing up in f****** up situations? • If I lost my life would anybody care?

They also have clear reasons for writing about self.

Richard Wright	14-year-old Applicant
• Then I sat down. Why do that? My problem was here, with me, here in this room, and I would solve it alone here or not at all. • All my life I had been full of a hunger for a new way to live . . . I picked up a pencil and held it over a sheet of white paper . . .	• Can't talk to God cuz he either acts like he's not there or he just doesn't wanna hear my prayer; • This sh** makes me mad that's why I start to write . . .

Another young male, a 16-year-old junior from a single-parent household, defined himself as a "CNN Politics junkie" in his application as he wrote about what drives and motivates him. He opted to submit a writing sample of his own choice, about which he stated, "What I have chosen to submit is a short, rhetorical piece I wrote on why Barack Obama's book *The Audacity of Hope* matters. Each of my classmates chose his own book; Obama's was my personal pick. His eloquence and character have made him my dearest idol." The excerpt from his piece that resulted from a Books Matters Project at his school follows.

What drives and inspires people comes in many a vehicle. Often times, I find myself sitting at home, struggling to complete a homework assignment, and I think of scenes from "Akeelah and the Bee," trying to emulate a young girl's academic persistence. Or when I feel weak and powerless, I'll find myself replaying scenes in my head from "Die Hard," imagining I had the strength and perceivable immortality of John McClane. What reading *The Audacity of Hope* has allowed me to do is admit yet another vehicle into my garage of inspiration—a space which will never run out of room.

Coming into the Books Matter project, I savored the fortune of having already assigned a great deal of ethos credit to the author of the book I elected—Barack Obama. At the time of his book's publication, Obama was not yet the United States President-elect, nor is it even certain that he had began to devise a presidential campaign strategy—the year was 2006, and Obama was a U.S. Senator from Illinois. When the significance of publication date begins to matter is when I go back to evaluate the integrity and credibility of my author. While *The Audacity of Hope* is very much a drive-in to see Obama in a sentimental, family-oriented light, it is also a vehicle Obama uses to showcase some of his potential presidential policies: most of them FDR-esque, that is, "for the people." Those policies alleged to benefit the masses, like tax breaks for the working class or natural production and reservation of energy, are the same policies on which are the most difficult to follow up. Assessing Obama's presidency five years later, I can see those same policies he promotes in the book employed, and, with that, I realize one reason *The Audacity of Hope* matters to me is that it coerced me into recognizing a genuine, ethical respect for Barack Obama.

I probably would not have chosen a senator-written book if politics didn't matter to me. I grew up with a distinct affinity for politics, starting with inquiry as simple as, "Mommy, why did Clinton get fired?" to eventually arrive where **I am now: an avid *New York Times* reader, a CNN Politics junkie** That political curiosity found its place not only in helping me to understand some of the complex political ideas Obama brings forth here but also in eliciting the political analyst inside me who assesses both the quality and sensibility of various political theories. I felt informed enough to legitimately either agree with or critique Obama's political rhetoric.

The worlds of these two boys seemed far apart—one a "CNN Politics junkie," the other contemplating suicide. I was curious what would happen if I brought them together to write about their "Blackness" wrapped in its heterogeneity. I did not view the content of one piece of writing as more valuable and significant than the other. I was more curious about how these young males were using their pen to define themselves and what factors informed their definitions. These young males would be placed in a writing environment with another African

American male adolescent who wrote poetry about butterflies and another who described how his ancestors did not raise him "right talkin' smack and then they fight generalizations in a fried chicken nation and takin' cool-aid vacations."

Although I led an African American Adolescent Male Summer Literacy Institute, I was not looking for "one kind of Black" or "the same kind of Black." A historical analysis of the writings of African American males suggests the absurdity of this approach. In *We Who Are Dark* (2005), Tommie Shelby writes about the long-standing philosophical conundrum—the meaning of "Blackness." He places "Blackness" into two categories—thin conception of Black identity and thick conception of Black identity. He offers the following definitions:

- **Thin conception of Black identity**—Blackness is a vague socially imposed category of racial difference that serves to distinguish groups on the basis of their members having certain visible, inherited physical characteristics and a particular biological ancestry (p. 206).

- **Thick conception of Black identity**—This includes a thin component, but always requires something more. Thick Blackness can be adopted, altered, or lost through individual action. This concept of Blackness treats identity as heritage, nationality, a set of values, and as a form of kinship. It may involve the use of "brother" and "sister" to affectionately refer to fellow Blacks (p. 207).

The poems on page 25, written by two of my students, represent an example of each conception of identity.

Thin Conception Author From Institute 3	Thick Conception Author From Institute 3
Equals • Black • White • Spanish • Latino • Italian • Hispanic • It doesn't matter what race you are • If we work together we all will go far	**Is Black Important?** • Is Black important? • You tell me • The struggle of my race has come so far • So it is important isn't it? • No, wait yes • You know what? • I don't know any more • I want to be confident of my answer • Yes • Discrimination will no longer corrupt my thoughts • I am sure now • The answer has been there forever • **Black has always, is, and forever will be important**

 FEARLESS VOICES © 2013 by Alfred W. Tatum, Scholastic Teaching Resources

Author From Institute 2	Author From Institute 2
Paint Me the Color of a Nation	**Black People**
Black, but my skin is brown	To you, Black people means people with brown skin.
I was born in America, not an African Village.	For you do not know where we come from or where we've been.
My ancestors went from Africa to Egypt.	<u>We are</u> of Sub-Saharan African descent
I could be Egyptian American.	14% of the world is what we represent
Everyone else knows where they are from.	A small number that we fought so hard for during the African Diaspora
Irish, English, French, Canadian	<u>**Strong descendants**</u> of the Zulu Nation that is why we continue to tour around the globe to spread Shaka's blood
One Nationality	But you're not Black.
I seem to have two.	It's ok if I wasn't understood.
Maybe I was born in two countries at the same time.	
Africa was a name given by a conqueror.	
The true name of the slab of rock is unknown, God given.	
Native Americans are the ones native to America.	
African Americans are those brought from Africa to America.	
But I was born here.	
Why separate Americans?	
Who was born in America?	
Scientists always want to name things.	
White? That's a pure color. You look a bit red yellowish white to me.	
Black is a solid color.	
But man, look at my skin.	
It's brown.	
Clearly someone is confused.	

This is why I often find it problematic when high school English teachers ask questions similar to one I heard during the reading of *Black Boy*—"What do you think it was like to be a Black boy in 1945?" This type of question only trains students to think about "Blackness" in superficial ways. This type of questioning extends beyond classrooms to the political sphere. Herman Cain, a Republican presidential candidate during the 2012 primaries, explained that he was not "that kind of Black," but a "businessman Black" when asked why he did not protest during the Civil Rights Movement. Although it made for great political theater, the questioners viewed "Blackness" in a very superficial way, a superficiality I wanted the young males I worked with to challenge.

Beyond Superficialities: First Day of Each Institute

On the first day of each Institute, I greeted the young males with a handshake, a computer to use for the duration of our five-week writing session, and a copy of the Institute's preamble. At 10 o'clock exactly, I directed them to stand and read the preamble in unison with me. I then had each young male read the preamble individually before directing them to memorize it within 24 hours. Each subsequent day we recited the preamble without viewing the written text. I called on one or more of the young males to recite the preamble verbatim after we recited it as a group. I then ask them to explain its meaning. This was the opening structure of the Institute and for each session.

Each day of the Institute I went through a brief PowerPoint presentation. The goal is to have the young males writing within 30 minutes of each three-hour session; giving them more than two hours of writing time each time we met. The PowerPoint Slides used on Day 1 from Institute 4 are at left.

I then asked the young males to share what they know about the author of the two poems from their writings. I also asked them to select one line from each poem and share their views about that line. I found that asking them to select one line and express their views about that line engaged them more than asking them to share their views about the entire poem. This was also important as a way to set them up for commenting on each other's writing and dissecting pieces of each other's text line by line. The PowerPoint slides were used to frame the day's writing.

The key to getting the young males to write each year and to understand how one writes to define himself was placing my own writing before them and opening it up for critique. The first writings I placed in front of them across the four Institutes along with the rationales I provided to them for writing each piece are below.

Our Strivings

by Alfred W. Tatum

Will someone take our text
along with them?
Are we standing ready to write
at a moment's notice?
(Living with our eyes and
mind open.)
Can we carry our lives through
our pens?

Poetic Broadside

by Don Lee – Haki Madhubuti

America calling
negroes
can you dance?
Play foot/baseball?
nanny?
cook?

They call me monster.

They call me beast.

I just want to be human.

Give me the language to put my voice on record

Before I cuss somebody out

Then they will call me an inarticulate, foul-mouth fool

Doomed by another descriptor.

Help!

Rationale for writing: I am seeking the language to define who I am so that I can put my voice on record. You will create poetic broadsides that focus on issues you believe affect young males of color across the diaspora. Start with your own community and expand the lens.

Measuring Up

by Alfred W. Tatum

How many strands of hair do I have on my bald head?

How many thoughts are there in my empty thinking?

What do you make of the word love I have tattooed on my right arm that shot a glock

What ACT score do I need to get my mind off the block where I once S.A.T as a child

Everybody wants to find the right instrument to measure me

To see if I am becoming what others want me to be

How about this?

I changed my lil bro's dirty diaper

Combed my sister's nappy head

Tucked my mother in her seventeen-year-old bed with no headboard

And I borrowed a roll of toilet paper

Before heading off to ninth grade to score a perfect 100 on my algebra test

What's my score on the algebra test?

Then, I went to English and scored 97% on my quiz

Right after I borrowed a shirt from my boy so I wouldn't look dirty in front of Monifa

Who sat in the chair behind me

Don't ask me about the quiz and some stuff I can't even remember

Because my mind is clouded hoping she didn't see the hole in the back of my shoes

What's my score on the English quiz?

Then I had to change in P.E.

With the same dingy drawers

That I am ashamed to have anyone see over the back of my pants

No drooping jeans for me

I keep going because I want perfect attendance

What's my score for P.E.?

All the time I am thinking how I can change things

For my lil bro and nappy headed sister

Hoping my mother lives long enough to see their successes

And so my dad will be proud of them when he sees them again

I am trying to be the glue and hold it together

But I am so conflicted, restricted

Trying to measure up to people who do not know how to measure me

With their strange instruments

Off to history class to turn in my paper about democratic ideals in a global society

That I worked on all night just to get it right

After listening to more bad news on the news about me

I hope Mr. Johnson uses the right rubric on the paper to get it right

My perfect and near perfect scores are adding up

But so are the sores

Where is the instrument that captures both?

Maybe being measured is not a good idea

I think I am going to focus on measuring up

But I am sure someone would like to know how to measure measuring up

I'll let them figure that out

While I go home to feed my lil bro and nappy headed sister.

Rationale for writing: I wrote this piece because it is time that we use our words to measure ourselves in an environment in which strange instruments are used to (mis) measure our total humanity.

Tethered

by Alfred W. Tatum

Concreted streets
Signed by black bodies
Sounds of childhood
Replaced by death whispers
Broken and fragmented souls
In need of an autopsy

Rationale for writing: My broadside focuses on the notion that many young Black souls are tethered to a storm that refuses to release its grip.

Jumpsuit Timeline

by Alfred W. Tatum

Leaning toward the right
Weighted down
With strangled cats
My first drug
Teacher who kicked me out of 1st grade
A beat down at eight
A fight with the principal at ten
Caged on my twelfth birthday
A new present for the system
Crying at 17 with one day left before the State says I'm a man
I'm a GOOD GOOD BOY who defaulted his mother's love
Tomorrow among the men who will prey on my youth
That I surrendered

Rationale for writing: Writing is often needed to make sense of the complexity that affects our being, doing, and acting. The above piece was inspired by a visit to a juvenile facility in Philadelphia where I asked young males to share their timelines. The image of the green jumpsuits on their young Black bodies still haunts me.

Preamble

We, the Brother Authors, will seek to use language to define who we are, become and nurture resilient beings, write for the benefit of others and ourselves, and use language prudently and unapologetically to mark our times and mark our lives. This, we agree to, with a steadfast commit-ment to the ideals of justice, compassion, and a better humanity for all. To this end, we write!

We, the brother authors, will seek

WHY WE ARE HERE

- To be courageous, bold, even heroic
  in our writing
- To be a part of a community of Brother Authors
- To exercise literary freedom
- To become urgent souls
- To put our voice and vision on record
- To become a student of humanity

YOU CARRY

- Your experiences
- Your world

OTHERS HAVE CARRIED OR CONTRIBUTED

- Research
- Words and voices
- Their experiences

PLATFORMS

- Defining self
  o Personal self
  o Cultural self
  o Gendered self
  o Economic self
  o Community self
  o National self
  o International self

- Becoming Resilient
- Engaging Others
- Building Capacity

AAAMSLI GOALS

- Each Brother Author will write a minimum of 30 pages of text over a five-week period including the following:
- Poetic broadsides
  o Black shorts (at least 2)
  o Children's story (at least 1)
  o First three chapters of your novel

Becoming the Architects of Our Own Lives

Without fail and with little reservation, the young men at the Institute began to write about their personal, cultural, gendered, economic, community, national, and international selves, initially from a deeply emotional space. It was as if they were anxious to write. An excerpt from one young's male piece is below.

"Even when nobody's with you, you still have a voice"

by Jamil Boldian

I'm sitting here in the dark without a voice

Everyone's left me standing without a choice

A choice to redeem myself with simple goals

Goals to challenge myself in victory where everybody goes

But who knows where I'll end up

A chance to survive in the world because it's rough

So you've got to be tough especially in my neighborhood

Where I had enough

Enough! I said to the little poor Black child

He was spooked and had to lay low for a while

Wow! I thought to myself as I wondering what was that sound

I heard of mines

How I would respond to it

What's my next line . . .

Another student, a 17-year-old, expressed his time-sensitive anxiety about writing as illustrated in two excerpts on the next page.

From the Voice of Words

by Joseph Shaw

So write I will, can't mark time until with vast knowledge still. Feelings of
wise men before me make visible their words so a deaf man can hear them.
Beautiful as midday, the words speak with fulfilling knowledge. Don't stray away
from the seemingly doomed fate of God. Use the way the mighty wind speaks
a mind of its own. Shown to this day barriers can be overthrown. The feelings
of the pen have spoken. Softly, the words shall appear—dangerous though. . . .
Tick. Tick. Don't let time run out. . . . Let our testimony be the pen.

From My Writing Shall Not Wait

by Joseph Shaw

Listening, soaring through the language world, trying to be great. I say out loud
my writing can't wait. It is a common thing in the world to say people hate what
they can't appreciate or even buy your stock shares before they inflate. **I speak
my mind, craving not to take my time.** I don't hold back, it's not just mere words
to me. It's what describes me as a human being by the ability to wrap the ideas
into the souls of other people.

These young males were becoming this generation's cultural bearers as they searched within
themselves for the next lines to write, seeking the lines with a sense of urgency. They also
expressed an unwillingness to "hold back" their voices if it meant providing a "more" accurate
portrayal of themselves. One of the young males suggested an adopted immunity taken by
African American males toward inaccurate portrayals. This is reflected in his piece, "Same old,
same old." I resonated with this piece because it reminded me of a poem I wrote a year earlier
after receiving a university e-mail alert about a crime committed by a young African American
males in the vicinity of the University of Illinois at Chicago, located near my office on the
corner of Harrison and Morgan. I coupled this experience with one when I, as a second-year
assistant professor at the University of Maryland, was pulled over by the campus police while
driving a large SUV on my way home around 10 pm after spending a late evening in my office
grading papers following a night course I taught. The officer let me go without apology after
I showed him my license, registration, and faculty ID (my modern-day manumission papers). I
juxtapose our pieces below:

Same Old, Same Old

by Donovan Wade, 13-year-old African American male

I walked into the store today

The store clerk looked at me in a strange way

I waited in line for this white guy in front of me

When it came to my turn the clerk said "I need to see some I.D,"

I walked down the street eating my newly bought chips and

The cops stopped me saying that a car was stolen and I happen to fit the description.

I entered a music store to see what albums I can see

A worker took me to the Dr. Dre "Chronic" album saying this is for me.

I was waiting at the bus station for a bus to take me home

The white guy next to me said "Please leave me alone"

I got back to my apartment building at 9:17

I saw another some other white and he looked at me mean.

I entered my apartment and my mom "Son what's wrong, looks like your day was rough"

I simply replied "Don't worry mom, just the same old stuff"

As I lay in my bed with sores on my feet, I ask

"Why the same stuff gotta happen to me?"

Crime Alert

by Alfred W. Tatum

5' 9"–5' 11"

armed robbery on the corner of harriSON and morgan

weight/wait 170lbs to 195lbs

this is another description of me

I'm in the police blotter although I teach at the university

I was pulled over at the university of merrryland/Maryland for driving a green sUv

Now, I am at ulc

the same mess is occurring

waiting to be pulled over because I meet the same PROfile

My phd can't even save me

I need to grow taller or lose some weight/wait

this will be my great escape

man, who am i fooling

genetics got me trapped in the quagmire

I am afraid to open the next e-mail alert

that's alerting me to be aware of myself

feeling like a criminal

although I've never committed a crime

I'll keep my knife in my pocket

just in case i decide to rob myself

ain't that a damn shame

While teaching African American males over the past years, I often shared that it was important that they did not capitulate to static images and stale ideas. I offered, "It's time to develop a new blueprint. The voice, missing in action, is a form of surrender." I shared the following poem with them.

Missing Architects

by Alfred W. Tatum

More than a million speeches and conference proceedings

Focused on the intersection of my Blackness and dangling manhood

They talk about me in hotel lobbies and national newspapers

I am thought about by think tanks

I am scorned in the comments section following a news article about me

I have even become profitable in the worst way

They are given vouchers and federal dollars to save me

From what, is not clear

Church leaders have profited

I have made a lot of careers at top universities by folks who "address" my need in print

Without addressing me

They don't even have my address or telephone number

No one has ever called my cell

There are too many architects at the drafting board

Without a clue

Without my blueprint

All leading to unintended consequences

Yielding the same image

My blueprint may help to make sense of it all

One line, one scribble at a time

This poem reifies the need of young African American men to write to define themselves without apology, becoming part of a long line of African American male writers who did the same.

Critical Questions to Consider When Supporting African American Males to Write to Define Themselves

1. How did writers historically use their pens to define themselves?

2. How do you wrestle with the complexities of writing about oneself and writing about one's ethnic identity?

3. How is one's humanity connected to his definition of self?

4. What texts can I use to illustrate the definitions of "Blackness" that are not superficial and proselytizing?

5. How do I support my students to explore language in its fullness to define themselves?

6. How do I create an environment in which different conceptions of "Blackness" are honored?

No, the real reason I had the breakdown is that I saw the system for what it was. I was going crazy in my head, trying to figure out how to get my kids out, to protect them from the system. I knew it was going to grind them down.

—From *Best Intentions: The Education and Killing of Edmund Perry* by Robert Sam Anson

CHAPTER 2

NURTURING RESILIENCE

In this chapter, I focus on writing as a pathway toward resilience. Resilience is defined as remaining steadfast in the face of destabilizing conditions. Resilience can also be defined as having more protective factors than risk factors. Risk factors are characteristics of individuals, their family, school, and community environments that are associated with increased delinquency, school dropout, and violence. Factors that counterbalance risk factors are called protective factors. Protective factors encompass family, social, psychological, and behavioral characteristics that can provide a buffer for youth. These factors mitigate the effects of risk factors. I discuss writing as a protective factor. I begin with a personal story.

> **KEY POINT**
>
> To write is to grow intellectually. Intellect is a tool of protection; therefore, writing is a tool of protection.
>
> —Alfred W. Tatum

Writing first became important to me as a 16-year-old junior in high school. I had to select a topic for my junior research paper. I decided to conduct research on the Ku Klux Klan. While preparing for the television show, "Know Your Heritage," I learned about the gruesome tale of Michael Donald, a 19-year-old Mississippian who was murdered by members of the United Klan of America in 1981. This is believed to be the last known lynching in the United States. I wanted to bring the Klan down, in part because I was spooked by the details of Michael Donald's murder. Two men sought to kill the first Black person they saw in retaliation for a jury verdict in which an African American was found not guilty for murdering a white person. Donald's skin color alone marked him for death. He was strangled to death. His throat was slit. He was hanged from a tree. For more about Michael Donald's lynching, see National Geographic film, *KKK: Inside American Terror: A Modern Day Lynching*: http://channel. nationalgeographic.com/channel/episodes/kkk-inside-american-terror/

As a high school student, I understood what it meant to be marked by skin color. During my sophomore year, I was placed in the back of a police car for the first time along with a good friend who eventually became the valedictorian of my high school graduating class. We

Me circa 1986 near the time I wrote my research paper on the KKK and the year I was placed in a police car for the first time.

were accused of snatching a woman's purse at the mall. In his puzzlement at being wrongly accused, my friend managed to find a small degree of humor in the situation that resulted in his slight laughter. One of the officers then uttered, "You won't think this is so funny when we drop your [expletive] off in Canaryville, a predominantly Irish-American neighborhood in Chicago that had a reputation for hostility towards African Americans. The assault against African Americans in this neighborhood dated back to the 1919 race riots in Chicago. The police officer threatened to offer us up as bait. We were released from police custody after the victim, who was waiting in the mall's security office, informed the officers that we were not the ones who snatched her purse.

The perpetrators of Donald's murder were convicted of criminal charges in 1983 and were found guilty in a civil lawsuit in 1987. This was the year I graduated from high school. One of the guilty men received the death penalty. Apart from a white man who was executed in 1913 for shooting a black man, this was the first time in American history that a white man received the death penalty for lynching an African American male. Lynchings of African American males had managed to survive for more than two hundred years without such a verdict. I was familiar with the history of lynchings because I lived in the Ida B. Wells housing project in Chicago. Ida B. Wells led an anti-lynching crusade in the late 1800s through the first quarter of the 1900s, the height of lynchings in the United States. This was the backdrop that led me to select my topic for my research paper. It mattered little to me that my paper was going to be graded by Dr. Thurn, a white male English teacher. I was writing for myself for the first time. I used my pen to drive my mission. This type of writing is now referred to as social justice writing (Christensen, 2000; Singer, 2006) in the educational literature. My research paper became the first piece that garnered my full investment.

Writing became a way for me to combat America's psychological grinder. The grinder for African American males, both overt and subtle, is difficult to escape. For example, I was approached by a white male, the husband of a literacy scholar at the annual convention of the National Reading Conference (now the Literacy Research Association) in Albuquerque, NM, in 2009, who asked me how I learned how to speak Standard English. I was a member of the NRC's Board of Directors at the time. Although I have no empirical or anecdotal evidence, I would bet that no other white or male member of the board who was born in the United States was asked or would be asked a similar question. I was marked. My response to the question was, "I was taught the same way your white daughters were taught." Our conversation ended abruptly. I refused to engage in his mythical "how did you beat the odds?" mindset.

Such a mindset places African American males in a psychological grinder. I was having a conversation with an African American male doctoral student who offered that he "beat the odds." I asked him several questions:

1. Are you blind?
2. Are you deaf?
3. Is your brain impaired?
4. Did your parents abandon you?
5. Were you denied access to free public schools and a free public library?
6. Were you sick or hospitalized for most of your childhood?
7. Did you live without shelter for the better part of your life?
8. Were you hungry most of the time?

He answered "no" to each of the questions. I then asked him to explain why he believed he beat the odds absent of the things that could have really made his life difficult. I guess when one hears something so often he comes to believe it is true until someone leads him to think differently. One of my goals during my Literary Institutes was to engage African American male youth in the rewriting of myths about themselves.

The psychological grinder pales in comparison to a physical grinder experienced by many African American males. In the epigraph of the chapter, the mother of a young man, Edmund Perry, expresses her concerns about her sons living under a system that has the potential to grind them down. Edmund Perry was an honor student from Harlem who graduated from Phillips Exeter Academy, one of the most prestigious private schools in the country. He was an honor student at Exeter who studied a year in Spain. His mother's nightmare of "grinding" was prophetic. Edmund Perry became a victim of police brutality when he was shot to death at age 17. He was not able to take advantage of his scholarship to Stanford University. Perry was killed in 1985, the year I was writing my high school research paper.

Edmund Perry, an honor student from Harlem who was shot and killed in 1985.

In each case—Michael Donald's, Edmund Perry's and my own—being

Black and male contributed to our being profiled across different geographical landscapes: Mississippi, Harlem, and Chicago. We could have become interchangeable pieces. Having supportive, loving parents did not insulate Donald and Perry from losing their lives. Vulnerability in their cases was not related to economic status or academics. It was related to Blackness and maleness in America's context. African American males in America have a "vulnerability quotient" simply based on phenotypic characteristics.

Although outraged, I was not shocked by an incident that occurred in Chicago as I was preparing this chapter, an incident that directly relates this vulnerability quotient. A trio of white male teens placed a noose around Joshua Merritt's neck because the Black teen was sending texts and Facebook messages to a white female, the cousin of one of the attackers. This criminal behavior, now considered a hate crime, emerges out of a tradition of miscegenation laws in the state of Illinois that were enacted in 1829 and repealed in 1874. Here is an explanation and excerpt from Illinois:

> In 1829, the "ACT respecting free Negroes and Mulattoes, Servants, and Slaves" was revised. . . . Finally, it was declared illegal for any negro or mulatto to marry any white person. Section 3 also declares any such marriages null and void, and anyone seeking to be married in violation of this law was to be given no more than 39 lashes and imprisoned for not less than one year. Any official who presided at the marriage of different races faced a fine of not less than $200 and would be ineligible for any future office in the state. By 1845, it was illegal for people of differing races to cohabit. Those who did so were believed to be living in an "open state of adultery and fornication." Anyone convicted of violating this law was subject to a fine of up to $500 and imprisonment for not more than a year. If this was not a sufficient deterrent, "for the second offense the punishment shall be double, for the third treble, and in the same ratio for each succeeding offense."

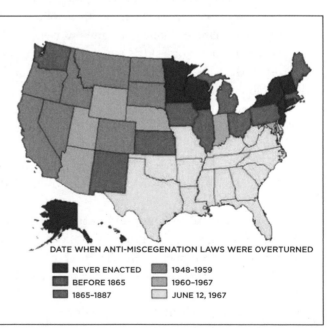

DATE WHEN ANTI-MISCEGENATION LAWS WERE OVERTURNED

- NEVER ENACTED
- BEFORE 1865
- 1865–1887
- 1948–1959
- 1960–1967
- JUNE 12, 1967

The map captures the states in the United States with miscegenation laws.

Mary Mitchell, a columnist for the Chicago Sun-Times, wrote about the hate crime in the article, "If Young Whites Are Still Shaking Nooses, We Have a Long Ways To Go."

If young whites are still shaking nooses, we have a long ways to go

By MARY MITCHELL mmitchell@suntimes.com January 27, 2012

When I look at my 11-year-old grandson, I see the young man he will become.

Already an exceptional scholar and gifted athlete (he is an inch and a half from towering over his 5-foot-4 mother), and he rocks the same playful dimples that make his father's serious face handsome.

I take in all of this whenever I watch this grandson at play with teammates who don't look like him. For as long as he has been in school, he has been the only dark face in the crowd.

If he's ever been concerned about being the "only one" in the group, he hasn't shared it with me.

Right now, his life is just like the lives of his friends. They play soccer and basketball. They sing in the choir. They huddle over science projects. He's slept over at a classmate's house. The classmate has slept over at his.

Once, in the heat of a close soccer game a white kid on the opposing team called him the N-word. But the soccer moms demanded a reckoning from the team's coach. The matter was handled with an apology and forgotten by season's end.

Still, I worry about him being in an environment lacking in diversity. His mom is convinced I worry too much. But she went to diverse schools. She was never the only one.

What will happen, I ask her, when he discovers girls?

In response, she rolls her eyes as if I've gotten into a time machine and sent it back to the 1950s.

I wish I had.

I wish the accusations against Matthew Herrmann, an 18-year-old at Brother Rice High School, and two other white teens were something my grandson read about in a history book rather than in a newspaper.

The trio is accused of putting a noose around Joshua Merritt's neck because the black teen was sending texts and Facebook messages to the female cousin of one of the attackers.

Herrmann has been charged as an adult with battery, unlawful restraint and a hate crime. The two other teens are being charged as juveniles.

According to Merritt, he was invited to meet up with Herrmann and his friends at the Beverly home of a Cook County state's attorney's employee where the attack allegedly took place.

Apparently, once Merritt got comfortable, his attackers pulled out the noose and put it around his neck. When Merritt tried to flee, his attackers allegedly blocked his way. After Merritt managed to get away, a 16-year-old accused in this incident followed him to the bus stop and threatened him with a knife. Merritt said he was told to "stop talking" to the boy's cousin.

Because Merritt was not beaten, the tendency will be to dismiss this despicable incident as a tasteless prank.

But Black people do not play with nooses.

The noose is a symbol of racial hatred and intimidation and hearkens back to a time when Black men were hanged from trees just for looking at a white woman.

Merritt may not have been physically harmed, but if white teens put a noose around his neck, he was horribly humiliated.

Worst yet, Merritt was apparently lured to the Beverly home under the guise of friendship. Merritt obviously didn't think Herrmann and his alleged co-conspirators meant him harm.

The African-American teen told reporters he had been friends with Herrmann since his freshman year at Brother Rice.

Merritt thought the teens had a "trust with each other," which is how he put it when he spoke to reporters.

So much for trust.

You can never know what is in someone's heart. But if the facts are true as presented by Merritt, this attack appears to be rooted in racial intolerance.

That is what worries me most about my grandson's situation. Right now he is innocent, and I don't want him to think racism is behind every social slight.

Yet I also don't want him to be naive. Racism still exists. I had hoped the next generation would be a lot more tolerant when it came to race than my generation.

But if young white teens are shaking nooses, we still have a long ways to go.

Although vulnerabilities are not unique to African American males, some fester because of long-standing myths birthed in America's bosom. Others are based on contemporary circumstances. Parents who enrolled their sons in my Literacy Institutes expressed concerns about the following:

1. Their sons' limited exposure to African American history
2. The fact that their sons attend a high school with a predominantly white student population
3. The fact that their sons are being raised by a white mother and have limited experiences with other African American males
4. The fact that their sons never have an African American male teacher
5. The fact that their sons live in a household without their fathers
6. Their sons' lack of consciousness
7. Their sons' need to improve their writing to apply for colleges and universities

Becoming Resilient

I worked with African American male youth to increase their resilience quotient. To do this, I first had to understand the risk factors contributing to feelings of vulnerability. I asked the African American males to respond to the prompts below as part of the application process and throughout the Literary Institutes:

- Too often young people surrender their life chances before they get to know their life choices. Use your pen to make sense of this dilemma.
- Identify one myth about African American males. Provide a writing sample in which you address the myth.

An analysis of their writings (e.g., poems, short stories, children's stories) indicated that African American male adolescents wrestle with tensions/issues of vulnerability through multiple lenses.

Racial Lenses	African American Male Adolescents' Writings
Intra-racial lens Writing informed by tensions/issues within the race	**Is this what we have become?** After all the fight and struggle for freedom Is this what we have become Killing and fighting one another like animals We should take charge and do something with our lives If not, what's the point of being free It can do no good for me

FEARLESS VOICES © 2013 by Alfred W. Tatum, Scholastic Teaching Resources

Racial Lenses	African American Male Adolescents' Writings
Interracial lens Writing informed by tensions/issues across races	**The Friend of the Nine** The sound of my mother wakes me up, as I get dressed I literally stumble on my thought once again thinking about Little Rock . . . I then run for the first bus I see. Not knowing that Elizabeth Eckford, one of the nine, was sitting in the back of the bus, frightened. She gets off the bus but is confronted by a white mob, when I see this I hop off the bus also. I try to push away the evil eyed white folks. She then ran to the back of the school, probably trying to go in through the back door. There's nothing I can really do except to cry her name while praying the mobs don't follow her . . .
De-racialized lens Writing not specifically informed by tensions/issues of race	**Darkness** Deep in the jungle with nothing at all NO light to see my way to safety Cold and wet I feel dead Laying down Breathless and darkness covers my face Praying for the day I find the light.
Ultra-racial lens Writing informed by tensions/issues related to historical and contemporary occurrences that divided people by race. The language in these writings are laden with racist references (e.g., the use of *Nigger*)	**The Writer** Donte sat on a haystack. He was looking down at something. His left hand seemed to be moving something. Suddenly, the doors to the place he was in swung open. A Caucasian woman appeared; a whip in her hand. Her face was bright red from anger. Her veins showed from her neck. "Donte!" she yelled. "You stupid nigger! I told you to be in the cotton fields a long time ago!" "I . . . I . . . . I'm sorry, Mrs. Dakota," Donte said. "It won't be happenin' again."
Post-racial lens Writing that attempts to move beyond tensions/issues of race	**In the Ring with Blake Blackburn** "As an African-American, do you feel as if you are better than your opponents?" Gregg asked. "Ummm . . . I don't think race would have anything to do with skill levels, it depends on the time you spend perfecting your skills," said Blake.
Trans-racial Writing that attempts to capture the connections between people of African descent	**Black People** We are of Sub-Saharan African descent 14% of the world is what we represent A small number that we fought so hard for during the African Diaspora

These lenses emerged from their writings; it was not forced upon them. For example, I did not ask the students to write from a post-racial or intra-racial lens. Instead, I asked them to identify socially important issues, conduct research on the Internet on these issues, and write pieces in a specified amount of time (usually, one to one and a half hours). The range of their writings was impressive and very difficult to typecast.

Research to Write from a Point of Strength

The goal of writing for resilience was not to incite the young males to become consumed by risk factors or subscribe to a victim's mentality, but to find strength to write beyond the risk factors. I encouraged them to write from an empathetic stance if they did not view themselves as vulnerable in their brief time on Earth. I did not want to turn my happy-go-lucky 11- and 12-year-olds into sour, cynical souls. To help them understand how African Americans wrote for resilience, I offered the following on a prepared PowerPoint presentation during one of the Institutes.

Oh Heaven! I am full!!! I can hardly move my pen!!! And as I expect some will try to put me to death, to strike terror into others, and to obliterate from their minds the notion of freedom, so as to keep my brethren the more secure in wretchedness, where they will be permitted to stay but a short time. I shall give the world a development of facts, sheikh are already witnessed in the courts of heaven.

—*Featured Brother Author, David Walker*

He was **no soft-tongued apologist,**
He spoke straightforward, fearlessly uncowed,
The **sunlight of his truth** dispelled the mist,
And set in bold relief each dark hued cloud,
To sin and crime he gave their proper hue.
And **hurled at evil what was evil's due** (p. 6).

—*Paul Dunbar wrote this about Frederick Douglass in* The Collected Poetry of Paul Laurence Dunbar.

If literature has taught me anything, it is that essentially you have to always go sub-surface, you have to go deep within yourself in order to be comfortable with yourself . . .

Four things
1. "I would never again, ever apologize for being Black."
2. "If I take this position I have to know who I am."
3. "If I am going to contribute, then not only must I read, but I must write."
4. "I decided that I was going to go into the idea business."

—*Featured Brother Author, Haki Madhubuti*

Planning

Activate some knowledge by prewriting and reflecting.
Research tools
- Almanac
  www.infoplease.com/almanacs.html
  www.fadmonster.com
  www.worldalmanacforkids.com
  www.myteachertools.com/almanacs.php
- Thesaurus (word choice)
  www.thesaurus.com
  Do the words suit the context?
  Jot down relevant experiences

Facts and Names: *Option*
- Fill in Research and Prep Chart (see Appendix A)
- Identify elements (names, facts, places) that are essential to get your point across.

FEARLESS VOICES © 2013 by Alfred W. Tatum, Scholastic Teaching Resources

I then distributed the completed chart to demonstrate how to use facts to create titles and sentences for their pieces.

Writer's Research and Prep Chart

Facts	Title	Sentence(s)	Name/Place
African Americans are 12.5% of the U.S. population.		"I am just little more than a dime" struggling within a dollar.	
Chicago has the second largest African American population in the U.S.			
U.S. President's salary is $400,000 per year. Members of Congress make $174,000.		How did the $169,000 man cast his vote? I wonder what the $169,000 man has to say about the 37 percenters.	
There are 2.8 million residents in Chicago. African Americans constitute 37% of Chicago's population. What % of African Americans are there in my school?	Traveling Between Contexts Multiple Worlds		
32.9% of African Americans own their homes.			
U.S. Senators from Illinois Dick Durbin Mark Kirk	"Double D"— A note to my senator		
1 out of every 133 U.S. residents is behind bars.	Caged Nation Iron Bar Nation		
The U.S. has more people in prison than any other country.		African American males have the highest incarceration rate in the United States.	
_____%* of African American males are incarcerated. ___ % of African American males between the ages of 25 and 35 are incarcerated.			

* Invite the students to research and fill in the blanks; these percentages shift from year to year.

I told the young males that "part of taking care [to pen a quality piece] as a writer requires conducting research." I also told them that research lends itself to not only writing from an emotional space but from a cognitive space. I would challenge my students on the facts of their writing. One student had a piece with the words, "all Black males." I then asked him to give me the number of Black males in the United States, in Illinois, in Chicago. He had no clue. Therefore, I informed him that he couldn't use "all" again until he conducted research.

I shared my research chart for the poem, "Hut Boy" in a PowerPoint slide, and discussed how having facts allows one to write with greater authority about an issue. I told them how I struggled for two days to write the piece for the young Haitian Brothers living in huts. This piece was sparked by a comment made by the artist Wyclef Jean during a Black Entertainment Television (BET) awards show. He mentioned, "There is no excuse, I was born in a hut." I decided to write to the Hut Boy.

Haiti

Hut Boy

- There was no common birth certificate before approximately 1990. *Peasant (peyizan) is a category of citizenship on the national birth certificate form of rural blacks.*
- Poor blacks in Haiti are referred to as stupid beasts.
- La Saline—one of the largest slums
- Haitian names—Jean, Phillipe
- *Tout moun se moun—Haitian proverb meaning every human being is a human being
- Toussaint L'Ouverture—Led the Haitian revolution to defeat the French, Spanish, and English Armies
- Jean-Bertrand Aristide—first democratic elected leader

Hut Boy

by Alfred W. Tatum

Without common birth
I sit in my hut of hope
Unphased by my scorched feet
My mind remains in tact
Tout moun se moun
Speaks our Haitian-born leader
As he takes up the cross for liberation
My dark soul rebels
Reminding me that
I am a good person
Phillippe, they will say one day
You are the leader of this nation's revolution
Toussaint, would be proud
Hail to you, our son of La Saline (slum).

I mentioned that writing should raise the consciousness of the reader if the goal is to nurture his resilience, and informed them that writing should contribute to their own elevated consciousness. I offered, "A writer should not be the same person after writing a piece as he was before he wrote it." I noticed a shift in their writing and consciousness after they completed the writer's research and prep charts in relationship to socially important issues they had never written about before. Within an hour, the young males began to write about the U.S. military, Blacks in Hockey, the African Diaspora and Shaka Zulu, the Little Rock Nine, their U.S. Senator, and the strained relationship between Germans and Jews, among other issues. Below are several samples of this writing.

WRITING SAMPLE 1

Minority Majority

2.4 million BLACK Military Veterans in the U.S.,
the most of any minority,
yet WE only make up 12.5% of the U.S. population.

While others dodged the draft of WWII,
We fought for a country that treated US wrong.

In 1866, the *Buffalo Soldiers received second class treatment
and were given the worse assignments,
but had the least desertion rate of any regiment.

Twenty plus Buffalo Soldiers have received the Medal of Honor,
the utmost of any other military unit.

The last Buffalo Soldier named Mark Matthews,
died in 2005, at the age of 111.

These soldiers make me exceptionally proud of my heritage
and I salute every last one of them!

* *Buffalo Soldier was a name respectfully given to the African American cavalries during the 1800s by the Native American Kiowa tribe.*

WRITING SAMPLE 2

Black People

To you, Black people means people with brown skin.
For you do not know where we come from or where we've been.
We are of Sub-Saharan African descent
14% of the world is what we represent

A small number that we fought so hard for during the African Diaspora
Strong descendants of the Zulu Nation that is why we continue to tour
Around the globe to spread Shaka's blood . . .

Words of resilience started to appear in their writing as illustrated by the underlined parts in the sample writings above. I was particularly struck by the following piece by a young African American male who reenvisioned himself as Heinrich, a teen who was part of Germany's so-called "master race," to capture the difficulty of remaining steadfast in the face of overwhelming odds. He completed his chart on the Holocaust before writing the short story, "The Torture of Inhuman Souls."

WRITING SAMPLE 3

The Torture of Inhuman Souls

by Preston Davis

Hearing about something and seeing it are two completely different things. And hearing and seeing something is completely different from hearing it, in the sense that you weren't there to hear it when it was actually occurring. Am I making sense? I guess it doesn't matter since nothing makes sense. So how do you make sense of nothing? I've asked myself that question every time I've awakened from a night's sleep, or a day's sleep, notice I didn't say a good night's sleep. And there nights are even worse, I would say it's beyond my imagination, but I don't imagine, I witness. Do we have to die so others can live? Excuse me, correction, do THEY have to die, so that others may live.

Not others, we, do they have to die so that WE can live? I think I got it right that time. I stare into the darkness, hoping to find an answer in the crevices in my uniform. The Swastika on the arm represents a belief, my belief. Wait, whose belief? If it's mine then the folds in the jacket must represent the wavering of the very belief the garment is meant to represent.

OOOooowwhwhHhhhaahahhhhhh!!! That's what it sounds like.

The wailing doesn't stop, how can it? The way they're treated, excuse me, the way WE treat them, I can't blame them for yelling. Though, I'm surprised they have the strength to.

This place is like a graveyard, all I see are people who've handed over life, animate, dead bodies, not even dead bodies . . . but skeletons with skin. Did we do this? Why? Why are they not fit to live and we are? He told me we are the perfect race and that all others need to be eradicated, but . . . if we rid ourselves of the imperfect, assuming we are perfect, then won't we be normal? If there is no superiority factor, nothing to be above, then how can we call ourselves perfect if there is no longer a sense of imperfect?

I don't believe it matters anymore, within this camp, it's hard to believe that anything could matter. I could say that, and yet I'm well taken care of, from the outside looking in, the mirror reflects whatever stares at it though. I don't expect anyone to understand, anyone who CAN'T understand, the ones who haven't witnessed, or have been through the tunnel, can never tell what the inside TRULY looks like.

"Heinrich, you done writing in that journal of yours yet," asked Reinhard. "We're on patrol, and for God's sake put on some clothes man."

As I sat in my chair I looked around the dark room, at my desk my lamp and journal served as my only escape, my bed unmade, nailed on the wall was a hangar with a Nazi uniform hanging from it.

"Those, they are no clothes of mine . . . give them back to Hitler, they're his clothes."

"Now listen here you!" Reinhard rushed me and knocked me out of my chair, then grabbed me by the throat and shoved me against the wall. If it hurt, which it did, I sure as hell didn't show it.

"Not again here with this Jewish crap. I don't care if you are my nephew you're gonna get this crap right if I have to beat it into you, you are part of the master race, don't go having sympathy for those unworthy of life!"

There it was again, "master race." Is it because of the slick blonde hair on my head that fell unto my face, or is it because of my piercing blue eyes that glared at my so called uncle with discontent?

"Just because you deem them unworthy of life doesn't mean I have to be the executioner!" I shouted almost too loud for anyone NOT to hear.

My uncle must have noticed the same thing because he gutted me one.

"Shut up, do you want the whole camp to know of your weakness," he spat.

"Compassion is not a weak _____"

"Shut up, you're becoming a worthless wretch just like your mother!"

"Has this life changed you so much that now you'd even insult your own sister, your own blood, isn't she's considered an Aryan as well!?"

His face softened, if just a bit, no one else would have noticed it, but I've been around long enough to.

"You've still got a lot left to see, boy," he said while dropping me. "Go on and get that uniform on and you don't have to be the executioner; just don't be the savior."

"If I were to stand by and do nothing, I wouldn't be the savior, but I would be the executioner the same if I had done it with my own two perfect hands . . . contradiction is the very nature of humans. Be it imperfect or perfect it's a part of our blood, it flows through us as natural as the flowers bloom in the summer. I'm not wrong to question the ideals of anti-Semitism, you are wrong not to."

"Be that as it may, we don't even have a choice anymore."

"What do you mean?"

"I mean, you've still got a lot left to see, boy," he said as he left the room.

I could have sworn I almost heard a tiny hint of despair in his voice.

The group of young males stood and applauded the 15-year-old who wrote this piece. This young man expanded the boundaries of writing and thinking for the other young males in the Institute, giving them permission to be deeply human and Black or Black and deeply human.

Writing, Resilience, and the Weight of African American Fathers

Although the young African American males displayed evidence of becoming resilient through their own writings, the reality of the weight of missing fathers crept into their writings across the four years that I led the Writing Institutes. The pain of not having a dad at home was obvious in a number of pieces. Missing fathers was an ever-present psychological grinder, increasing the vulnerability quotient. Look at the pieces below.

I Hate You

by Kendrick Washington

For not being able to see
The times when you
Asked me to tag along
I shrugged it off
I let you be
You chose your path
You lived your life
Instead of being free
You chose to fight
I hate you
For not taking a stand
Instead of doing all the drugs
You could of changed
Into a man
And realized that life is not a joke
You kidded your way
And even died with the smoke

And I'm glad that you choked
It didn't matter to you
That's why your spirit was broke
So much for thinking things through
I hate you
For not being a brother
Dishonoring your mother
And not being a father
And running away
From all your fears
God thanks for the courage
You soon will pay
No word clashing
As I try, not to shed a tear
I hate you
For being trapped underneath
In another's person treasure
Your prize was defeat
And the prize you think you've won
Is not winnable
You sucked up all the joy
Ruined everyone's fun
I hate you
For dying before you ever got a chance to know
Or watching me succeed,
Or maybe grow
Into what I have become
Why?
Because I have earned it
Unlike what you haven't . . .
I hate you
For being a liar
Your legacy is gone
Being burned in the fire
And as I realize
I wouldn't want to become a PIECE of you
It's finally over,

It's finally through . . .
I hate you
For not being able to see
The times when you
Asked me to tag along
I shrugged it off
I let you be
Your absence burned inside
That's what was killing me
I hate you . . .

If I Were That Child

by Thelonious Stokes

If I were that child, I would have his father
I would share the inspiration to be just like my dad when I grow up
I would be able to run to his bedside when I have a frightening dream
I could be shown how to talk to a woman, or toss a ball
But I am not that child.
If I were that child I would be praised by my teachers for being the perfect student
I would be able to dream of a perfect life
I could be a strong influence
But I am not that child.
But since I'm not that child, **I am able to overcome! I am not that child, I am not**
    that child, I am not that child! But if I were that child . . .

One of the authors, a 15-year-old, resolved to hate his father while the other, an eighth-grade student, wondered how his life would be different if his father were present. I did not overlook the pain caused by an absent parent. The data are clear that African American boys are at greater risk of not being reared by a father in their households. They are also unlikely to have an African American male teacher in preK-12. This is real abandonment from their fathers (or those men whom they resemble), which they have to wrestle with. Still, they have to find resolve, becoming part of the next generation of fathers to raise their own sons. In the next piece, I combined my love for baseball and for fatherhood to write a short story that pays attention to two of the platforms discussed in this book—nurturing resilience and engaging others. The short story had two goals:

FEARLESS VOICES © 2013 by Alfred W. Tatum, Scholastic Teaching Resources

- Reconnecting young males with their fathers
- Encouraging young males to accept their fathers when they return

I started the following short story with an "unapologetic" bang although I rarely use profanity in the works I share with students.

My Daddy's Shrine

by Alfred W. Tatum

My momma always told me that my daddy ain't shit, but I still decided to love him. I'm his seed and I carry his name. It's been three years since I last saw him. It was a perfect day. I remember waking up early on my tenth birthday. The blinds failed to block out the morning's sunlight that crept into my room. The ray of light stretched like a rope across the tiny bedroom that I shared with my little brother, Fergie. I dressed quickly when mom told me that daddy was on his way over to take me to the game. I heard the horn and I rushed downstairs. Big Gib, with a cigarette hanging out of the corner of his mouth, was sitting in his new Chrysler. He looked perfect to me. I was excited to go to the north side to see the Cubs. Kids in my neighborhood lost interest in the game; the parks are now empty. It is rare that I get a chance to wear my jersey with the number 37 on the back, another gift from my father. He's fourth generation and I am fifth generation.

My great grandfather moved to Chicago from Philadelphia in the 1920s. Philly was the Black Mecca of baseball for a long time. As long as I can remember, dad always talked about the famous left-hand catcher Willie "Gibson" Wells, who played for the Grays. Stealing second base on Willie Wells was like trying to steal a piece of fresh meat from a cage of hungry lions. He went by the name, "It just ain't goin' happen." The depression forced great grandpa to move to Chicago. He got a job slaughtering hogs. Although he never played again after slicing off two fingers and a thumb in an accident, he never could get the game out of his head. His stories were passed down to me. I began to love the game like my dad.

Big Gib knew I loved the sound of the train going through the tunnel. He parked the car close to the ballpark and we rode the El train the last few miles. It was crowded. He held my hand tightly as we snaked through all the people with Cubs and Brewer jerseys. We were special, the only two fans with jerseys from the Negro Leagues—the Homestead Grays and the Kansas City Monarchs.

"Today, we're sitting in the left infield box seats right over the dugouts."

I couldn't believe it.

"It's not every day you turn ten, Gibby."

My name rolled off his tongue with such affection. The Cubs were up by two runs, and I was glad that I did not have to share my cotton candy with Fergie. We were having our own special day until the bottom of the third inning. This strange lady walked up to Big Gib and kissed him on the lips. A boy who looked my age followed her. I hadn't noticed the two empty seats until they plopped down next to us. He was wearing a jersey like my dad with the number 37. There were now two Grays vs. one Monarch.

"Introduce yourself Gibby. Robby knows all about you."

How could he know all about me and I know nothing about him? I was wondering if Big Gib shared all the same stories about the number 37. Big Gib told me, "It carries weight to wear that number on your back. Only 37 Negro Leaguers made it to baseball's Hall of Fame." He told me that the 37 hall of famers were not better than the rest, but they were able to breakthrough. He always called me his "Breakthrough Kid." Now, there were two of us. He was sitting on Big Gib's right side and I was sitting on the left side.

The game became a blur as I stared at the 400-ft marker on the wall in centerfield. The innings went by quickly. It was the beginning of the seventh-inning stretch when I heard Big Gib say, "Time to stretch, sons."

"You mean son, right?"

"No, Gibby. Robbie is your brother. I thought it was time for you to meet him."

"I don't want to meet him. I wished you would have left me at home with momma."

"I will next time. You and your mother deserve each other."

"That's not nice, Big Gib," I heard the lady say.

I felt a tear roll down my face at the same time the fans around us started standing. A fly ball was heading in our direction. Big Gib managed to snag it out of the air with his huge hands.

"Can I have it dad?" Robbie asked.

"No, this is Gibby's. It's his special day."

It was hard for me to refuse the baseball. Robbie may have had the same jersey, but I had the ball. The Cubs, up by six runs in the top of the ninth, needed three outs to win the game. The crowd began pouring out of the stadium, but as always, Big Gib refused to leave the game until the final out. He believes leaving early insults the game and the players. I was ready to leave, but I did not want the day with my dad to end.

Cubs win! Cubs win!

"Honey, I will see you and Robbie later," my dad said.

He leaned over and gave the lady another kiss before grabbing my hand and leading me through the crowd. He was all mine again just for that moment at least. I had the ball to prove that I was the special son.

That was the last time I saw Big Gib. He called and sent me a card for my eleventh birthday. We talked for a few minutes on my twelfth birthday. I did not hear from him on my thirteenth birthday. Maybe, he forgot how to love me the way he used to, the same way we forgot how to love the game. I will be ready for him when he returns. Until then, the shrine I have in my room—the jersey, the ball, the ticket from the game, the glove, and his photo—will keep us connected.

Discussion of this short story afforded the young males the opportunity to talk about their fathers and fatherhood in general in an environment with other young males who were being raised by their fathers and other who were not.

I then shared three research charts I used to plan the story. To fill in the first chart, I read a book on the Negro Leagues. For the second chart, I reflected on my experiences going to baseball games. I used the third chart to plan the events, settings, and dialogue for the short story.

Chart 1: Baseball Game

Sounds	Smells	Sight	Feels
• Applause • "Seventh-inning stretch" • Crack of the bat • Delirious cheers	• Warm bread • Urine • Peanuts • Cotton candy • Coca-Cola • The tunnel • Bratwurst	• Crowds • Long lines • Concession stands • Cubs jerseys • Foul balls • The scoreboard • Pitcher's mound • Dugout • Old people • Beer man • Runners on first and second • Umpires • Infielder/outfielders • Pop-up hanging in the sky	Daddy's hand

Chart 2: Negro League Baseball vs. Negro Baseball League

Facts	Names	Teams
1885: The Cuban Giants formed the first Black professional team.	Satchel Paige	**Illinois Teams*:**
	Cool Papa Bell	Chicago American Giants
1883: Moses Fleetwood "Fleet" Walker joins the minor league Toledo Blue Stockings as a catcher.	Oscar Charleston	Chicago Brown Bombers
	Josh **Gibson***	Chicago Columbia Giants
	Monte Irvin	Chicago Giants
The first known baseball game between two named Black teams was held on September 28, 1860, at Elysian Fields in Hoboken, NJ.	Buck Leonard	Chicago Union Giants
	John Henry Lloyd	Chicago Unions
	Rube Foster	Leland Giants
	Hank Aaron	
By the end of the 1860s, the **Black baseball Mecca was Philadelphia**, a city with an African American population of 22,000.	Ernie Banks	Missouri Teams:
	Roy Campanella	**Kansas City Monarchs***
	Larry Doby	St. Louis Stars
	Willie Mays	St. Louis Giants
1920: On February 14, **Rube Foster organized the first Black professional baseball league** (Negro National League) consisting of eight teams: Chicago American Giants, Chicago Giants, Dayton Marcos, Detroit Stars, Indianapolis ABC's, Kansas City Monarchs, St. Louis Giants, and the Cuban Stars.	Jackie Robinson	Pennsylvania Teams:
	Leon Day	Harrisburg Giants
	Bill Foster	Harrisburg Monrovians
	Bullet Rogan	Hilldale Daisies
	Hilton Smith	**Homestead Grays***
	Turkey Stearnes	Philadelphia Pythians
	Willie Wells*	Philadelphia Giants
The Negro National League was absorbed into the NAL after the 1948 season.	Smokey Joe Williams	Philadelphia Stars
	Minnie Miñoso	Philadelphia Tigers
Minnie Miñoso was the last Negro League player to play in a major league game when he appeared in two games for the Chicago White Sox in 1980.	Buck O'Neil	Pittsburgh Crawfords
	Bingo DeMoss	Pittsburgh Keystones
	Fats Jenkins	
	Sam Jethroe	
37 members of Baseball's Hall of Fame played for a Negro League Baseball team.	Grant "Home Run" Johnson	

* Details selected for the short story.

Chart 3: Writing the Short Story—Charting Events/Settings/Dialogue

Describe an object in the room	The blinds failed to block out the morning's sunlight that crept into my room. The ray of light stretched like a rope across the tiny bedroom that I shared with my little brother, Fergie.
Provide a cause-and-effect statement	Kids lost interest in the game; the parks are now empty.
Recall the ending of an event	The crown began to pour out of the packed stadium.
Describe a person in a location	Big Gib, with a cigarette hanging out of the corner of his mouth, was sitting in his new Chrysler.
Describe your action	I was standing in front of the shrine to my father.
Write about an event leading up to a holiday/special event	I sent a letter to my father three months ago to remind him about our plans for the 4th of July.

The Complex Terrain of Writing and Resilience for African American Male Youth

What makes some African American adolescent males vulnerable and how they deal with their vulnerabilities are difficult to assess. The writings of the young males in the Institutes illustrated that while they are different, they are part of the Black male paint swatch wrestling with similar issues. It is clear from history and the residual effects of racism that it is difficult for one to dress his way out of Blackness, be elected out of Blackness, talk his way out of Blackness, or submit a resignation out of Blackness. The ongoing crisis narrative about young African American males in the United States, often filled with vitriol, has a tendency to place young Black males in America's grinder. Writing for resilience serves as a buffer to the grinders discussed throughout this chapter. Nurturing the next generation of socially conscious writers require that we give them permission and encourage them to become intellectually aggressive with their pens so that writing becomes a bridge to resilience.

African American male adolescents must learn to engage in an inward search to tackle society's most pressing problems, particularly if these problems contribute to the suppression of the young men's humanity. They must learn to take counsel from the desert rock that advises them to listen to their voices to recapture that which is lost and to move from being vulnerable to being resilient. This idea is captured in the poem below.

The Desert Rock

by Alfred W. Tatum

Its odd shaped stared at me

Seemingly bothered by my troubled stance

And my strange isolation

In a place reserved for rocks and losers

I was out of place for sure

Not knowing how I ended up here

But the rock tempted me to talk

Sharing a conversation only reserved for a gOD I had long abandoned

Silly I know, but that rock opened its mouth

And asked, "What?"

I kneeled beside it to whisper my sacred thoughts

"I am scared to go on

Too weak to surrender

Can you help me?"

That damn rock just stared at me

For six hours and 14 minutes until the sun went down

I walked out of the desert never to return

With a rock that forced me to listen to my own voice

Renewed—to find all that was lost

I am concerned that the young male who had the noose placed around his neck will need to find his strength as he moves forward in an environment that reminded him that he was Black. I am also concerned about my own 16-year-old son, who could have easily been the noose-bearer, an interchangeable part, as I was when I was a teen. Becoming resilient can be summed up in the words of a young male who wrote, "I have been through everything, good times and bad, but it's not over, and I am going to keep fighting to the end." His writing will protect him if he continues to listen to his own voice. On Guard!

Critical Questions to Consider When Supporting African American Males to Write to Become Resilient

1. How can we support students to write from a position of strength and authority?

2. How do we honor African American males' writings in interracial contexts, particular writings that are framed by interracial and ultra-racial issues/tensions?

3. Which texts, both contemporary and historical, are important to nurture the consciousness of African American male writers?

4. How can we support African American males to write to bring a daddy home, to stop a bullet, to challenge myths, to reduce high school dropout rates among them, and to protect their life choices?

5. How do we engage African American male adolescents with the pen so that they embrace writing as a tool of protection?

My life calling is to be a servant for the people, period.
Money, fame, status, personal achievements, and all
that means very little to me when pain and suffering are
still real on this planet. I am interested in the powerless
becoming powerful.

—Kevin Powell, activist, poet, journalist, essayist, editor, hiphop historian

CHAPTER 3

FOR MY BRETHREN: ENGAGING OTHERS

In this chapter, I focus on writing to engage others or writing "to awaken my afflicted brethren" (Hinks, 1997). Peter Hinks was a lecturer of American history at Yale University and served as associate editor of the Frederick Douglass Papers when he wrote *To Awaken My Afflicted Brethren*. When describing his research, he wrote:

> *This book is about how David Walker (discussed in the introduction) compressed all that experience and knowledge into one great and unprecedented effort to goad an exploited people into uplift their understanding of themselves and smashing the slavery that was blighting their lives. His Appeal was the instrument of that uplift and his cultivation of a covert communication network in the South, the vehicle for delivering it. The Appeal is a masterpiece of exhortatory writing whose impact—psychological and social—on contemporary African Americans can only be compared to the impact that Thomas Paine's Common Sense had on white patriots of revolutionary America. (p. xiv)*

KEY POINT

Loving others imbues our leadership with hope and possibility and builds our capacity to help.

—Alfred W. Tatum

Walker's *Appeal* is a must-read text for understanding the role of writing to engage others. I read this text before the beginning of each Summer Institute that I hosted from 2008 to 2011. Engaging others is defined as bringing one's contemporaries into the fold to strive for a better humanity for oneself and others. This was the case with the *Appeal* and *Common Sense* as reflected in the quote above by Hinks. My journey as an educator began with the pen of two of my contemporaries, both of whom I knew only through their words. I was moved to change my life because of their words.

As an undergraduate finance major at Northern Illinois University in 1990, I received a wake-up call in the form of a newspaper article. Engaging in my customary newspaper reading as I traveled to class on a bus, I came across, "A Different Brand of Education: Programs Trying to Reclaim a Generation of Black Youths," published in the Chicago Sun-Times. In the article, Haki Madhubuti, a poet and teacher, was quoted as saying, "It is the responsibility of men and women, but primarily men, to deal with the problems of young Black men." (The article is reprinted on the next page.)

My dark hands began to shake. School failure was not part of my experience as a young male. I had to do something. The Chicago Public School system and other school systems across the nation were failing or hosting the failure of young African American males. I had not considered becoming a teacher until that moment. Instinctively, I got off the bus and began to look for the College of Education. I discovered that it was adjacent to the field house where the university's men's and women's teams played their basketball games. I had never paid attention to the building that sat just south of the field house's parking lot where I'd parked my car on numerous occasions. The idea of becoming a teacher was foreign to me. But I've kept the newspaper article all these years to remind me why I chose education as my vocation. Sadly, the same article could be written today.

While rereading the newspaper article before writing this chapter, the words, *"will undertake a controversial experiment,"* stood out to me. I am reminded of how I was introduced as a speaker for a group of teachers in a suburban school district in a blighted Illinois community. The speaker offered, "He's here to help us with the *Tyrell Johnsons* (name changed here) of the world. You know who I am talking about." The teachers nodded in agreement or uttered words of understanding during the introduction. On that day, *Tyrell* became the representative of all African American male youth. His name became symbolic of a particular imagination. Unfortunately, Tyrell was not there to tell his side of the story. I was asked to function as a stand-in. Tyrell, however, could have provided a personal, more accurate depiction of his schooling experiences using his own words if he was given the appropriate supports and afforded the space and opportunities. Without his voice, he becomes a subject of experimentation with educators scrambling to figure out what's best for him. When educators ask me, as they often do, why young African American males engage in certain behaviors, I often respond with the question. *Have you asked the young males?*

A Different Brand of Education: Programs Trying to Reclaim a Generation of Black Youths

October 14, 1990 | By Karen M. Thomas, Education writer

At Jensen Scholastic Academy on Chicago's West Side, about 30 Black boys will soon attend special weekly classes intended to build their self-esteem, provide them with male role models and teach them about African history.

In Milwaukee next fall, the public school system will undertake a controversial experiment (italics added) by opening an elementary and middle school geared specifically towards nurturing and educating Black males.

In Washington, a group of Black men have adopted a local public school and become surrogate fathers to boys growing up in poor neighborhoods and single-parent homes.

These are some of the new and unique responses being made to a problem that has long plagued inner city public schools: the inability to reach and teach great numbers of Black boys, who then go on to unsuccessful futures marred by joblessness, poverty and crime.

The crisis is helping to destroy an entire generation of young Black men- unraveling the fabric of once-vibrant Black communities, forfeiting the future of Black families, and placing great social and economic burdens on the rest of the American population.

A plethora of alarming statistics bear this out: more than half of Black males enrolled in Chicago high schools never graduate; 29 percent of Black men between the ages of 20 and 29 spent time in the Cook County Jail last year; and Black men nationwide stand a 1 in 21 chance of being murdered.

Now, a wave of new programs aimed at guiding Black boys through the perils of growing up and helping them make the most of education is evident in many parts of the United States. One key difference about the new effort is that an increasing number of Black men are signing on to nurture the next generation.

Many have lost faith in the ability of ill-equipped public school systems to inspire young Black males, set them on the right path and provide them with the skills needed for jobs, citizenship and personal satisfaction.

Tens of thousands of Black men and women are fanning out in communities across the nation, devising programs in public schools, churches, community organizations, businesses and universities, according to educators and Black community leaders.

"A great number have taken it upon ourselves to impact positively on our communities," said Haki Madhubuti, a nationally known, Chicago-based poet, essayist, teacher and publisher.

"It is the responsibility of men and women, but primarily men, to deal with the problems of young Black men," Madhubuti said. "We're about doing that." His recent book, "'Black Men; Obsolete, Single, Dangerous?" offers strategies.

At the heart of many efforts are education programs steeped in African and African-American history and culture, which advocates insist is an effective method to strengthen self-image and build self-esteem.

About two dozen Chicago public schools have adopted or are considering setting up so-called Afrocentric curriculums.

Charlene Porter hopes that her 6th-grade son will be chosen as one of the 30 mostly 7th- and 8th-graders being selected for the weekly image-building sessions at the Jensen school.

A single parent and member of the school council, Porter said she has had difficulty finding role models for her 10-year-old.

"He hasn't even had a male teacher," she said.

"When he got to the 4th grade, he drove me crazy. I could tell his self- esteem was real low. I cried through it. I'm just hoping that he's chosen."

One of the more intriguing programs is called Rites of Passage, in which Black men use traditional African rituals and principles to mark stages of growth and development-seeking to provide boys with a cultural context and the inner resources needed to resist the deadly temptations of urban ghettos.

"It helps a person understand who they are, all the way from the beginning of time, and when that happens it creates interpersonal power," said Reuben Harpole of the Center for Urban Community Development at the University of Wisconsin in Milwaukee.

"Once you know who and what you are, no one can stop you from reaching your goal," said Harpole, who next month will teach a course on the Rites of Passage approach at Malcolm X College in Chicago.

Another program is Concerned Black Men Inc., a national organization that has developed a mentorship program called Project 2000. Students meet and work with successful Black men who can serve as long-term role models.

The adults are committed to working with the same youngsters until the year 2000, from which the name is derived.

Public schools are especially targeted because a majority of Black boys appear doomed for failure as early as kindergarten in school systems that have low expectations for them, isolate them in slow-track or special education classes, and suspend them at greater rates than other children, according to several recent surveys and studies.

The words *"will undertake a controversial experiment"* stood out because historically, African American males were victims of experiments. Some of the more widely known or written about experiments are the 40-year Tuskegee syphilis experiment that ended in 1972 which afflicted injury on more than 600 African American men; and the 20-year Holmesburg Prison experiments in Philadelphia, written about in the book, *Acres of Skin: Human Experiments at Holmesburg Prison* (Hornblum, 1998), in which prison inmates, many African American men, were used as human guinea pigs to test several products that included toothpaste, deodorant, shampoo, skin creams, detergents, liquid diets, eye drops, foot powders, and hair dye. Contemporary practices that I view as school-related experiments, ones that do not require the consent of the students, but have a real effect on African American males include:

1. State takeover of schools
2. Mayoral control of schools
3. Reconstitution of schools
4. School closings
5. No Child Left Behind legislation
6. Race to the Top legislation
7. Charter School movement
8. Small Schools movement
9. Test prep
10. Standards-based practices
11. Curriculum mapping
12. Best practices
13. School consolidation
14. Common Core State Standards

The designers of each of these efforts neglected to engage the voices of African American male adolescents, or neglected to consider the flaws of each of these experiments in a timely manner after each failed to reverse the reading and writing outcomes for many of these young males. Many of these experiments range from five to ten years, long enough to study their failures before the next experiment is instituted. One of the experiments, school closings, had a positive correlation with increased violence in Chicago among African American males as they were forced to travel across neighborhood boundaries to attend different schools.

Although he was writing on a different topic, I find the words of Henry Highland Garnet, the first colored man to speak in the National Capitol in the 1880s, fitting to describe these experiments. He offered the following in "A Memorial Discourse," (Dunbar, 2000): "In theory they were right; but their practices were inconsistent and wrong" (p. 69). While there is more success by school reformers and policymakers to establish school-based expectations and targets for improvement, identifying and establishing literacy practices that lead to increased engagement or accelerate the reading and writing of African American male adolescents has remained elusive in modern-day contexts that ignore historical precedence. I wrote the following poem to capture the sentiments of these experiments.

Human Guinea: Subjects Without Consent

by Alfred W. Tatum

They never asked me
Enrolled
Probed
Diagnosed
Charted
Given new names (at-risk, vulnerable)
Will the benefits outweigh the risks?
What happens if the experiments fail?
Government protection?
Resurrection?
Rejection?
No recipro(city)
In my city
Quite gritty
My grandmother called my dad a human guinea
Sounded safer than a rat
A creature targeted for extermination
I laughed when I was a child
Now fuming as an adult
Because my son is now third-generation guinea
He has become ideal for research
In elementary and secondary labs
To gauge his response to extreme conditions
I am just waking up to see
After removing the blinders caused by my own participation
In an experiment
Without my consent

Engaging Our Young Brethren

My research, in which I have invited the participation of African American male adolescents, shows that these young men provide valuable insights into their schooling experiences, and direction for increasing their participation in reading and writing experiences (Tatum 2000, 2008). Honoring the voices of "my young brethren" was essential. The phrase, "My Brethren," was used often in early Negro writings that appeared in books, pamphlets, and broadsides from 1760–1837 as Black male authors wrote to improve the living conditions of free Blacks and to struggle for freedom and the advancement of Black people (Porter, 1995). African American male writers made brotherly appeals to:

1. Encourage other African American males to follow

2. Have other African American males wrestle with favorable and unfavorable truths

3. Hail African American males to accept changed realities

4. Encourage African American males to act on new understandings with zeal

5. Have African American males embrace vital principles

Several examples of African American males striving to engage others with their writings— that is, appealing to their brethren—are in the table below.

Author/Year	Text/Year	My Brethren "Appeals" Engaging Others	Type of Engagement
Prince Hall	A Charge Delivered to the Brethren of the African Lodge (1792)	Thus, my brethren, I have quoted a few of your reverend fathers for your imitation, which I hope you will **endeavor to follow**, so far as your abilities will permit in your present situation and the disadvantages you labor under on account of your being deprived of the means of education in your younger days, as you see it at this day with our children . . . (p. 67)	Physical engagement involving changes in actions
Jupiter Hammon 1787	An Address To The Negroes in the State of New York (1787)	You must suffer me now to deal plainly with you, my dear brethren, for I do not meant [sic] to flatter, or omit speaking **the truth, whether it is for you, or against you**. (p. 316)	Psychological engagement involving changes in thinking
William Hamilton—First president of the New York African Marine Society	An Oration Delivered in the African Zion Church (1827)	My brethren and fellow citizen, **I hail you all**. This day we stand redeemed from a bitter thralldom. Of us it may be truly said, "the last agony is o'er," the africans [sic] are restored! No more shall the accursed name of slave be attached to us—no more shall *negro* and *slave* by synonymous. (p. 97)	Psychological engagement involving changes in thinking

FEARLESS VOICES © 2013 by Alfred W. Tatum, Scholastic Teaching Resources

Author/Year	Text/Year	My Brethren "Appeals" Engaging Others	Type of Engagement
Joseph Corr	Address Delivered before the Humane Mechanic's Society (1834)	It remains then, for us, brethren, **to be up and doing; to put our shoulders to work;** to say to the great "mountain" of prejudice, by faithful perseverance and active energy, "Be thou removed," and instantaneously it disappears, before the spirited efforts of practical exertion. (p. 149)	Physical engagement involving changes in actions
James Forten, Jr.	Minutes and proceedings of the First Annual Meeting of the American Moral Reform Society held in Philadelphia (1837)	Let us sir, for a moment, contrast the difference between the literate and illiterate man. The one resembles a beautiful edifice, adorned and fitted up for occupation; the other an unfinished building abandoned by the slothful labourer; the materials are there, but [not a finger is raised to touch them; the straw is there, but no bricks are made]; and instead of carved frames, and richly moulded cornices, the wood remains in its rough, unturned state, without beauty, comeliness, order or symmetry. . . . My brethren, disguise ignorance as you may—cover it with all the adornments that fancy or art can suggest— still, through all that gorgeous apparel, may be seen its utter destitution of the one thing needful—the renovating, soul-cheering, **vital principle** of education. (p. 233)	Psychological engagement involving changes in thinking

Structuring Brotherly Appeals

Engaging others was one of the platforms used to ground the writings by African American adolescent males participating in the Summer Literacy Institutes. A young male from one of the Institutes taught me that writing to engage others cannot lead to "death ear construction." He was suggesting the writing should invite others to listen to your message. He told me that my writing was too angry and that I gave others license to dismiss my words. He assessed a particular piece I wrote as "counterproductive writing" during the time the young males were encouraged to critique my words. The original and the revision are in the table below.

Original	Revised
Questions	**Questions**
Why do you keep asking me so many questions?	Why do you keep asking me so many questions?
Who gives you the right?	Who gives you the right?
Your strange ways are irritating.	Your strange ways are irritating.
Let me ask you a question.	Let me ask you a question.
Why do you keep asking me questions?	Why do you keep asking me questions?
No more questions.	No more questions.
Answers only.	Answers only.
Now, do you still want to talk?	**Now, let's talk.**

He taught me that writers must take care to avoid getting in the way of what they are hoping to accomplish. If the goal of the piece was to have others engage in a collaborative conversation to support African American males instead of interrogating them with questions, he offered that I needed to revise the last line. I believe it is a much better piece based on the student's critique.

The student's advice was great because there were several times during the Institutes when I had to pen a piece to appeal to the young Brother Authors. For example, I overheard a young male laughing at his mistreatment at a Subway restaurant. I asked the young male if he purchased the sandwich after his mistreatment. He said, "Yes, I was hungry, but I made him give me what I wanted." He offered that he paid his money for a little extra that came along with being mistreated. In preparation for our next meeting the following day, I penned the piece at right, using his Subway experience, which contrasts allowing disrespect and honoring one's full measure of self.

No More (Sub) Ways

by Alfred W. Tatum
Inspired by R.B

Subsistence
　Full existence
Subpar
　Rising Star
Subjected
　Respected
Substitute
　Resolute
Subhuman
　HuMAN
Subway
　My Way
I am hungry, but you can have your
　sandwich.
I think I will make my own.

African American Males Making Their Brotherly Appeals

On the third day of each 15-day Summer Institute, I invited the young Brother Authors to engage others with their pens. I charged them to write their *last stand/call to action/deathbed broadside*. I instructed the young males to reflect on an experience that they could use to teach the rest of us a lesson, informing them that they were the change agents they needed. I told them that they would write for the benefit of others and ourselves as reflected in the Institute's preamble. The third day was foundational for the young males to engage others throughout the rest of the Institute as they also considered the other three platforms—defining self, nurturing resilience, and building capacity.

I used the following introductory slides during year four to help the young males conceptualize what it means to write to engage others.

Day 3—Last Stand/Call to Action/Deathbed Broadside

Brother Authors,

As the first week of the Institute comes to an end, we will write for the benefit of others and ourselves. To do this, I ask you to reflect on some experience that you can use to teach the rest of us a lesson. I offer a broadside below that captures the first time I was placed at gunpoint at age 11 (4015 days after I was born) in the Ida B. Wells housing projects. This experience and others, mostly positive, shaped my decision to become an educator. We are the change agents we need. Things will not change until . . .

Until . . .

by Alfred W. Tatum

Four thousand and fifteen days from my first breath
cornered by the brown brick fearing death
Invisible in broad daylight
The wide-opened eyes closed shut by dull beginnings
Could not see me/himself
Because of what he was (mis)taught
Confused
Distraught
Blood continues to drip

On the inner-city asphalt
Until . . . Until . . . Until . . .

The Young Brother Author penned a piece yesterday with the line "They say . . . we have rooms for our sluts."

How do we chop down that perception in America's imagination of young black males?

I wrote a broadside last year that connects to the need to support women with the unbearable burden of raising young brothers without the support of fathers.

Men must handle their affairs to recover all that has been lost and increase that which has been gained.

Men Affairs

by Afred W. Tatum

Spewing forth from blood-soaked sperm
Consigned to a raucous life term
I dare stand idly by
To watch another sister die

Her breasts have been scorched
Her nipples ripped away with steel
Her soul cries out to the brother
Who fails to hear her appeal

She raises another alone
It becomes the burden she bears
The dullness of her soul
Castigates men who know not their affairs

Her acidic tears that flow freely
Because of the neglect she feels inside
Shake me at the core
My manhood once again denied

My sons will be raised by a man
This indeed I agree
My own life is a wake-up call
To be the man God wants me to be

The examples illustrate writing for physical engagement that involves changes in action—"blood will continue to drip on the inner-city asphalt until . . . ," and psychological engagement that involves changes in thinking—"my own life is a wake-up call to be the man God wants me to be."

The young males began making their brotherly appeals from various perspectives. The first example below captures how a young male used autumn to engage others psychologically about the roles of African American males in their own success or failure. He refused to accept that Caucasians can be blamed for the failures of African Americans. His writing stands in the tradition of sharing hard truths to engage others. His piece is below.

Autumn Message

by Joseph Shaw

Leaves float down wistfully unto me, eyes shuddering, I see blurs

They look like people I've known . . .

In the crisp grass I rest, is how it should be

A field of play abandoned by all, I hear the birds calls

They sound familiar like people I've known . . .

I can taste the fading light in the air as the sun goes in hiding

My body feels cooler by the second and while I inhale the color of the leaves

My own fades. I feel weightless as if this field of grass was a never ending cloud in the sky.

My thoughts are becoming hazy as the wind blows more of my friends before my eyes

They all speak to me as they pass; I have to tell them something

The trees that surround me in a tight ring lean over me, watching.

Oh wait, it's my family surrounding me, they've come to help me stand.

I don't have the strength.

I stroke the hair on my brother's head

It's grown a lot, I have to, I'll tell him.

"Listen . . . if you believe . . . that . . . Caucasians are the reason you can't excel . . .

     that they're stopping you . . . then . . . you . . . are a Caucasian."

Through strained breaths I state my final words, to no one, no one

But my friends and family and my little brother, with his Black mask on.

That just happens to look like leaves, trees and a raccoon.

I hope he heard me . . . in the autumn breeze.

The next piece deals with the vital principle of sacrifice. A young male invokes the idea that everyone needs to make sacrifices despite the fact that the "balance is forfeit" in the lives of some.

Life Shines in My Red Eyes

by Byron Mason

LORD FORGIVE ME, FOR I HAVE SINNED.

I have committed murder. I have killed half myself.

The doctor says I have Bi-Polar Disorder.

And my yin just isn't equivalent to my yang.

The balance is forfeit.

I was born with red eyes, and as such I will die with brown eyes.

I see sunshine and rainbows and trees and flowers.

I see moonlight and black skies and earthquakes and roots.

I've seen my other death and it comes in the form of

Flashing lights and red carpets and Nixon cameras and

Yachts and nightclubs and fans and money hotels and liquor and drugs and parties.

All acquired by the satanic blood defiled consumption from gold goblets

and sacrificing my super natural for things of material nature.

I have not the capacity to try and turn back now

And I have not the blessings of my crowd.

WE ALL MUST SACRIFICE SOMETHING.

But forgive me angel if I believe I've sacrificed too much.

I was misjudged but you have been unjust.

The next piece exhorts others to follow the example of an indefatigable spirit—the refusal to give up and live the courageous life. He encourages his brethren to "get into the fight," and he provides a model of resilience when he writes, "I have been hit so many times, you would think I have 7 lives."

Courageous Life

by a Brother Author

Live
We only have one life
So you have to live it right
What you can accomplish
Is definitely out of sight
Live your life
Stand up

Get in the fight

Don't be afraid to take gambles

Cause life is going to knock you down

So get up

And go another round

Use your god given talents

You have to be courageous

By the end of the fight

I guarantee you will knock life down

Out for the count

And you will love the sound

Ring Ring

The bell will ring

The feeling will overcome the sting

That you felt when life hit you back

I am still in the fight

I've been hit so many times

You would think I had 7 lives

Yup I am a courageous cat

But at the end God will help me leave life on the mat

The next piece, "Unspoken," was written to encourage African American males to pen original pieces and speak new thoughts as part of the battleground for their existence. The writer was fed up with "drunken slurs of the repetitive mouth." The only things that are unspoken are the things the young males neglect to write or speak.

Unspoken

by a Brother Author

Tonguing the drunken slurs of the repetitive mouth,

Losing yourself in your speech,

Listening to yourself talk . . . for the hell of it

You say everything . . . but it's really nothing at all

You're only saying what they want to hear,

Not what they need to hear.

Protecting the unspoken word,

The truth,

Their demise,

Your personal hell.

It can make or break this game you created.

The game with one golden rule:

Say nothing.

Hide the words lingering on your tongue,

they are the game changers.

The game with one player,

You.

I constructed the following chart to illustrate the socio-historical connections these modern-day African American males had with their "brethren" of the past.

Brother Authors	"My Brethren" Appeals Engaging Others	Physical engagement involving changes in actions Typing of Engaging
Endeavor to Follow—provide examples for others to follow	I am still in the fight I've been hit so many times You would think I had 7 lives	Psychological engagement
Hard Truths—discuss internal and external barriers to young African American males' success	Listen if you believe that Caucasians are the reason you can't excel that they're stopping you then you are a Caucasian.	Psychological engagement involving changes in thinking
Be Up and Doing—take some physical action	Let yourself be heard. Spoken words can do wonders. And, you'll never do anything if you just wonder.	Physical engagement involving changes in actions
Vital Principles—maxims to embrace and an ethos to uphold	We all must sacrifice something.	Physical and psychological engagement

Engaging Others to Change the Game

This generation of young males has the potential to write to interrupt the status quo if we engage them in the process. Instead, educators concerned about the literacy development of

FEARLESS VOICES © 2013 by Alfred W. Tatum, Scholastic Teaching Resources

African American males continue to fail to engage their voices. The writings of the young males I have worked with, the ones who taught me about writing as I taught them, make me hesitant to be the "official" stand-in for them. This is why I refused to accept this positioning for Tyrell in that blighted south suburban community. Writing creates a new comfort zone for these young men, a new comfort zone we should embrace in English and language arts classrooms in schools as well as places outside of schools. There are several benefits of moving out of the comfort zone as reflected in the student's writing below.

My Comfort Zone

by Dailyn Miller

I used to have a comfort zone where I knew I wouldn't fail.
The same four walls and busywork was more like jail.
I longed so much to do the things I'd never done before
But stayed inside my comfort zone and paced the same old floor.

I said it didn't matter that I wasn't doing much.
I said I didn't care for things like commission checks and such.
I claimed to be so busy with the things inside the zone
But deep inside I longed for something special of my own.

I couldn't let my life go by just watching others win.
I held my breath; I stepped outside and let the change begin.
I took a step and with new strength I'd never felt before,
I kissed my comfort zone goodbye and closed and locked the door.

If you're in a comfort zone, afraid to venture out,
Remember that all winners were at one time filled with doubt.
A step or two and words of praise can make your dreams come true.
Reach for your future with a smile; success is there for you.

Ideally, moving beyond the comfort zone that constrains the writings and lives of many African American male adolescents in many of our nation's schools across several decades will make us "Never Again" educators who fight against repeated experiments that lead to school failure for "our young brethren." This is captured in the following piece written by another African American male.

Never Again

by Nile Lasana

Never Again
Will we stand and relax
While our brother's life
Is being hooked on a string.

Never Again
Will we rest in bed
While our children in Africa
Suffer from not being fed.

Never Again
Shall we embark on our journey
With more failure than forgiveness
And the act of being inconsiderate than affectionate

The darkness of obnoxious behavior
Unacceptable aromas
Sour tastes

Life is a gentle cup
Hard work and dedication will fill our world up.

The writings of the young males who used their pens to engage others helped reshape their realities—both psychologically and physically. They became "contaminated writers"—writing against the contamination affecting so many African American males in this nation. I instructed the young writers to "bring it on" to engage young brothers who look like them and others who do not, in the interest of a better humanity. I shared the following piece with the young writers during Institutes 3 and 4:

Contaminate Me

by Alfred W. Tatum

From the Dark Continent

Not viewed as a fit

Measured my daddy's head

Stretched my mother's womb

Models of destruction

To separate my kin

You imperialist snobs

Your multilateral assaults

Now you make me think it's my fault

Hid the inflammatory print

Afraid that mental laziness will turn into a sprint

As I rush to hang your deceit and your lies

With opened eyes

Shaping a new reality

I am now contaminated

Bring it on!

Critical Questions to Consider When Supporting African American Males to Write to Engage Others

1. How can we support African American males to deal with hard truths in their writing? What are some clear examples of these truths?

2. What principles are vital to the striving and survival of African American males in schools and society?

3. How can we engage African American males with our own writing that leads to changes in action and changes in behaviors?

4. What intellectual and emotional pathways are critical for supporting African American males to write to engage others?

5. How do we respond when African American males attempt to engage us with their writings?

In years to come, I believe because I have armed them with the truth, my children and their children's children will venerate me.

—Margaret Burroughs, Artist and Writer

IN THE SPIRIT OF BUILDING CAPACITY

Writing has functioned as the United States' bellwether, as America's guide. For example, the preamble to the United States constitution was written with a great deal of thought about future generations. I underline a few words below that capture this orientation.

> *We the people of the United States, in order to <u>form a more perfect union</u>, establish justice, insure domestic tranquility, provide for the common defense, promote the general welfare, and <u>secure the blessings of liberty to ourselves and our posterity</u>, do ordain and establish this Constitution for the United States of America.*

The use of the word *posterity* was intentional. The justices on the U.S. Supreme Court continue to examine the intentions of the Founding Fathers when making legal decisions for cases that have reached the highest judicial court in the land. "What did the Founding Fathers mean when they wrote . . ." is still one of the justices' guiding questions as they interpret the constitution.

KEY POINT

Writing carries a unique burden for the writer, his contemporaries, and future generations, particularly writing that deals with socially and politically explosive phenomena such as race and Blackness in the United States. To write about such issues for future generations requires thoughtful analysis, courage, and a bit of luck.

—Alfred W. Tatum

This chapter is written with an eye toward the future. The focus is on writing to build capacity. Building capacity is defined as creating a foundation for future generations—in other words, agenda building.

Readying Their Pens for the Future

During the Summer Institutes, I gave the young males permission to use their pens to share their vision for the future in much the same way that many African American male writers before them have done. For example, James Baldwin wrote a letter to his nephew in his book, *The Fire Next Time*. The following was part of the letter:

> *Now, my dear namesake, these innocent and well-meaning people, your countrymen, have caused you to be born under conditions not very far removed from those described for us by Charles Dickens in the London of more than a hundred years ago. (I hear the chorus of the innocents screaming, "No! This is not true! How bitter you are!"— but I am writing this letter to you, to try to tell you something about how to handle them, for most of them do not yet really know that you exist . . .) (p. 5)*

He ends the text with the following:

> *And we are, at the center of the arc, trapped in the gaudiest, most valuable, and most improbable water wheel the world has ever seen. Everything now, we must assume, is in our hands; we have no right to assume otherwise. If we, and now I mean the relatively conscious whites and the relatively conscious Blacks, who must, like lovers, insist on, or create, the consciousness of others—do not falter in our duty now, we may be able, handful that we are, to end the racial nightmare, and achieve our country, and change the history of the world. (p. 105)*

A close inspection of Baldwin's writing reveals that he was attempting to break bread across racial lines to bandage the U.S. racial divide in 1963. He was attempting to make sense of the existing hostile racial context and the people's involvement in America's racial trappings as he shared a vision for the future. Baldwin's words still have resonance almost 50 years later. This is not a light accomplishment for any writer. However, I encouraged the young males to write with such strivings, to sharpen the potential for the longevity of their words. They were encouraged to give their voice to Black male strivings and Black male sufferings specifically, and human strivings and human sufferings writ large. The focal points on strivings and sufferings in their writings were in large part influenced by the written works of W.E.B. Du Bois. Reflecting on the life Du Bois, Tanya Bolden, in her book *Upclose: W.E.B. Du Bois* (2008), wrote:

William Edward Burghardt Du Bois never raised a visible empire in Africa, but he did make a name for himself in social science and literature. Without a doubt, he did the utmost to uplift his race, convinced that when people regarded as the least are raised, the whole world gains. And so, for seventy years, Du Bois had given voice to Black strivings.

Giving Voice to Human Strivings

I summoned the young males to steep their writings in a prophetic tradition that involved both internal criticism (i.e., focused on African Americans) and external criticism (i.e., focused on systems in which African American males exist) that would lead to a new cultural awakening similar to that of the Harlem Renaissance in the 1920s. Daryl Michael Scot, in his introduction to the lost manuscript of Carter G. Woodson titled *Appeal*, wrote:

> *In the arts and literature, African Americans dedicated themselves to producing and creating expressions that proved the humanity and equality of Black life. In Harlem and across the nation, a cultural awakening was taking place that would become known as the Harlem Renaissance. Du Bois had long hoped that African Americans would become recognized as "co-workers in the kingdom of culture," and this vision caught the spirit of Black intelligentsia. In music, art, literature, and the New Negro generation made itself known. (pp. xxix–xxx)*

As I mentioned in the introduction to this book, the Writing Institutes were started to nurture the next generation of African American male writers. The young males, although bold and unapologetic in their demeanor toward writing, were not sure if they were qualified to speak for the next generation because of their youth. I tried to convince them otherwise. I informed them that the intersection of experience and knowledge gives them the qualification to speak, particularly as they learn how to weave both into a mosaic of truth-seeking and truth-telling aimed at large human goals without neglecting their cultured and gendered realities. These young males needed to embrace the fact that they were living at a unique time in this nation's history and the world's history. They were attempting to heed a call for 21st-century strivings amid untold violence. Some of the young males were striving to become scientists in destabilized communities with declining economic bases. Some were attending newly formed chartered schools in a dizzying educational climate focused on educating the least served among us, changes yielding evidence of small academic upticks or no upticks at all. Others were being asked to express their love for humanity when they couldn't find love from their fathers. Others were just 12- and 13-year-olds who enjoyed Cartoon Network and looked forward to their first kiss. Still, I wanted them to be prophetic.

The poem below, "The Prophet in the Shadows," captures the basis of the summoning as I prepared them to write children's stories and other texts for the next generation.

The Prophet in the Shadows

by Alfred W. Tatum

How old do you need to be to be a prophet?

To begin to shake the shackles of colonized minds

To get at the truth through your writing

To exert untold influence on the history of the world

The simple irrefutable truth

To share knowledge that others value

That demands submission from those with inferior knowledge

How old do you need to be to be a prophet?

It was my hope that they understood that being a prophet is not based on one's age, but is based on one's capacity to create the fertile ground for the next generation to follow.

Creating Fertile Ground

The writings of African American males have served as a fertile ground for the development of consciousness and have been aimed at the removal of ignorance and sin, feelings of castrated manhood, servile dispositions, or planned separation based on race prejudice and practice, and acquiescence to small upticks in progress. For example, the following was written by a committee of African American males who delivered "An Address to the Colored People of the United States" from the Colored National Convention of 1848 (Mullane, 1993):

> But, fellow-country men, it is not so much our purpose to cheer you by the progress we have already made, as it is to stimulate you to still higher attainments. We have done much, but there is much more to be done. While we have undoubtedly great cause to thank God, and take courage for the hopeful changes which have taken place in our condition, we are not without cause to mourn over the sad condition which we yet occupy. (p. 110)

> Never refuse to act with White society or institution because it is White, or a Black one, because it is Black; but act with all men without distinction of color. By so acting, we shall find many opportunities for removing prejudices and establishing the rights of all men (p. 111)

As a young African American male, I was influenced by African American men and women writers who gave voice to Black strivings. I remember one poem in particular because I memorized it for an oratorical contest I competed in when I was in sixth grade. Dr. Margaret Burroughs, founder of Chicago's DuSable Museum of African American History and Art, penned a poem that was part of the curriculum I experienced as a student attending a public school a few miles to the north of the museum. She began with the question, "What shall I tell my children who are Black?" Her poem is below.

What Shall I Tell My Children Who Are Black

by Margaret Burroughs

What shall I tell my children who are Black
Of what it means to be a captive in this dark skin?
What shall I tell my dear one, fruit of my womb,
of how beautiful they are when everywhere they turn
they are faced with abhorrence of everything that is black.
The night is black and so is the boogeyman.
Villains are black with black hearts.
A black cow gives no milk. A black hen lays no eggs.
Storm clouds, black, black is evil
and evil is black and devil's food is black . . .
What shall I tell my dear ones raised in a white world
A place where white has been made to represent
all that is good and pure and fine and decent,
where clouds are white and dolls, and heaven
surely is a white, white place with angels
robed in white, and cotton candy and ice cream
and milk and ruffled Sunday dresses
and dream houses and long sleek cadillacs
and Angel's food is white . . . all, all . . . white.
What can I say therefore, when my child
Comes home in tears because a playmate
Has called him black, big lipped, flat nosed and nappy headed?
What will he think when I dry his tears and whisper,
"Yes, that's true. But no less beautiful and dear."
How shall I lift up his head, get him to square
his shoulders, look his adversaries in the eye,

confident in the knowledge of his worth.
Serene under his sable skin and proud of his own beauty?

What can I do to give him strength

That he may come through life's adversities

As a whole human being unwarped and human in a world

Of biased laws and inhuman practices, that he might
Survive. And survive he must! For who knows?
Perhaps this Black child here bears the genius
To discover the cure for . . . cancer
Or to chart the course for exploration of the universe.

So, he must survive for the good of all humanity.

He must and will survive.
I have drunk deeply of late from the fountain
of my Black culture, sat at the knee of and learned
from mother Africa, discovered the truth of my heritage.
The truth, so often obscured and omitted.

And I find I have much to say to my Black children.

I will lift up their heads in proud Blackness
with the story of their fathers and their father's fathers.
And I shall take them into a way back time
of kings and queens who ruled the Nile,
and measured the stars and discovered the laws of mathematics.
I will tell them of a Black people upon whose backs have been built
the wealth of three continents.
I will tell him this and more.
And knowledge of his heritage shall be his weapon and his armor;

It will make him strong enough to win any battle he may face.

And since this story is so often obscured,
I must sacrifice to find it for my children,
even as I sacrifice to feed, clothe and shelter them.
So this I will do for them if I love them.
None will do it for me.

I must find the truth of heritage for myself and pass it on to them.
In years to come, I believe because I have armed them with the truth,
my children and their children's children will venerate me.
For it is the truth that will make us free!

Burroughs's text is a part of a storied tradition of cultural and intellectual real estate designed to educate African Americans males beyond the suffocation of historical distortion. Whether intentional or unintentional, such distortions serve to maintain America's economic, educational, and racial hierarchy and the cultural, economic, political, and conceptual "minoritization" of African Americans (i.e., the cementing of being called minorities and feeling like minorities) in America's imagination.

Ideas in the poem—namely the lines underlined and in boldface type in Burroughs' text—are similar to the key principles for writing to build capacity that we adhered to during the African American Adolescent Male Summer Literacy Institutes. The participants were asked to write children's stories and other texts while focusing on the following:

- What do I say to young Black boys?
- What can I do [write] to give young Black boys strength?
- What do I write to help young Black boys win any battle they may face?
- What do I write to a Black boy that focuses on his full humanity?

I provide excerpts from the Brother Author children's stories below that illustrate how they responded to each question.

Questions	Excerpts from Brother Author Writings
What do I say to young Black boys?	Look into my eyes **With age comes wisdom.** **So look into my eyes.** **With every wrinkle in my face, another story lies.** I look at you and I see myself But in an immature state of mind So eager to enter the world But, not knowing what the world hides . . . My brother I beg you look into my eyes With every wrinkle in my face another story lies. DAMN IT!!!!! YOUNG BRUTHA LOOK INTO MY EYES!!!!
What can I do [write] to give young Black boys strength?	From "The Trolley Ride" "I'm ready, how was work today dad, it looked tough." "It always is buddy, but we always get it done, **a man always finishes what he starts remember that son."** **His words stuck with me, as if he was challenging me to do something.**

Questions	Excerpts from Brother Author Writings
What do I write to help young Black boys win any battle they may face?	From "Life's Path" **Give me the test. I bet you I'll pass with straight Fs** Future . . . Forward . . . Forever moving . . . Man, ain't that thought soothing.
What do I write to a Black boy that focuses on his full humanity?	"ZIPPY" "Someone rescue the queen!" a bee yelled. "No, rescue the two butterflies. They're more important!" screamed a butterfly. When the bees heard this they became very angry and both sides began to argue. While the two sides were fighting no one noticed how close the spider was getting to the queen and butterflies trapped in the web. **Zippy realized he was the only one that would actually do something**. All of a sudden Zippy flew straight at the spider. The spider tried to grab him but Zippy was too small and fast. Every time the spider tried to grab him Zippy was already somewhere else. Eventually the spider became dizzy and fell off his web. By this time, the angry crowd of bees and butterflies were silent. Then a giant roar of excitement came. Everyone was so happy; they hugged Zippy and told him he was a hero. **The butterflies and bees asked him what he wanted in return for saving their loved ones. All Zippy said was *peace*.** Today the flower patch is no longer divided. Bees and butterflies work together to pollinate the followers. They offered Zippy to become king of the flower patch but he said no. Zippy flew off into the forest finally feeling comfortable.

The Brother Authors inserted messages in their writings they felt were essential to one's human development and essential for young African American boys because these were messages that allowed them to remain steadfast at this point in their lives (e.g., a man always finishes what he starts), or messages they wished they would have heard (e.g., give me the test. I bet you I'll pass with straight Fs—future, forward, forever moving). Some of the young males heard opposite messages and wanted to provide a counter-narrative in their writings. This counter-narrative was also evident as they grounded their writings in the other platforms discussed throughout this text—defining self, nurturing resilience, and engaging others.

There is a real urgency to write and speak to young African American boys who are affected by the stigmatic trappings of turmoil in many urban communities throughout the United States. I was recently struck by a news account in a local newspaper that highlighted the theft of metal mailbox slots in a middle-class community in Chicago. The story highlighted how the layered assaults on African American males within their communities and outside of their communities lead to strange behaviors The incident stimulated the following poem in which I strove to give a reminder that we need to find the right words to share with "'young boys with hope'" before they become "young adults with self-hate."

Empty Slots

by Alfred W. Tatum

Mailboxes ripped from their slots
A few kilometers from the liquor store
Confuse the retired police officer
Who raised his sons to be righteous
But failed to talk to the young boy visiting his neighbor
He only told his son to watch out for boys like him
Trouble's weathervane
The boy looked at his dirty socks
And whispered to himself
Trouble you see
I guarantee its reality
Damn you old man and your son
I will be back at your doorstep
To claim what you own
Mailbox and all
Only if you knew what to say to the young boy with hope
Before I became a young man with self-hate

Writing as Agenda-Building

During the week I focus on the fourth writing platform, building capacity, I enter the writing space and ask the Brother Authors, "What is the agenda?" Each young male is asked to respond. I am often met with blank stares or half-smiles. Several young males ask me, "Is this a trick question?" I do not respond, instead insisting that each young male orally share his "agenda." The responses range from personal agendas (e.g., winning a track meet) to global agendas (e.g., ending wars). I then inform them that writing as agenda-building deals with the present, but is also grounded in a vision for the future. This type of writing is guided by, at minimum, two questions:

1. What do children/adults need to understand?
2. What do I tell children/adults?

The young men are then encouraged to use their writing as a form of real estate. I ask them to fathom the future and their words within that future as they write fiction and/or an informational piece or a combination of the two. This is not an easy task for young teens, but the focus repositions them as agenda builders. To help them understand how African Americans can write to build capacity, I offered the following on a prepared PowerPoint presentation during one of the Institutes:

> You will create a young agenda builder—young philosopher, young artist, young activist, young community worker, young poet, young dancer, young talker, young athlete, young politician, young ????—who is keenly focused on some issue.
>
> You will work with other Brother Authors to describe three events with your young agenda builder centralized in each event.
>
> I am so looking forward to meeting your young characters.

> Brother Author Aaron McGruder wrote:
>
> And I was very aware of how valuable that little piece of real estate in the newspapers had become when the so-called free press lost their minds and started censoring themselves. I knew on that tragic day that more tragic were to follow, and I made the decision that I would use my little space to scream out louder against the great injustices that the United States government was about to unleash upon the planet.
>
> —*From the foreword of* A Right to be Hostile

I also shared the following with the Brother Authors in preparation for their writing to build capacity:

> Let's not be apologetic for what we want for the generation that follows.
> A famous, now deceased educator, Dr. Benjamin Mays, asked himself the following questions during his youth:
>
> 1. How could I be free in this world?
> 2. How could I grow to my full stature as a man?
> 3. How could I walk the earth with dignity and pride?
> 4. How could I aspire to achieve, to accomplish, to "be somebody"?
>
> He offered, "As one of the disinherited Black boys, how could I know that a part of the country, the state, and the nation belonged to me too? How could I exist?"
> Let's pen children's stories for the next generation of young boys so that they smile, grow, laugh, and love as they make their trek toward their teen years and manhood.
> We will write children's stories for those who come after us. Think about the young brother and sister sitting in the classroom, bedroom, or library, bored because they are struggling to find a book that resonates with them. Let's write for them using colorful words and rich language. Help them smile, laugh, feel warm, get excited, or get lost in their imaginations. We can also write to empathize with them and show them that we care about their young pains.

I read a preamble that contained the following words before moving out of their way so they could write:

> We live in a world where millions die from easily preventable diseases and still more face hunger as a daily fact of life. We are locked inside a worldwide economic system that dispenses crumbs and extends privileges to a relatively small number, while forcing billions to seek desperately for work that more often than not _numbs the mind, crushes the spirit_ and _destroys the body_ . . . .
> We walk through our days in a world where _the lives of countless children are ground up and destroyed_ . . . as victims of poverty and humiliation . . . _their potential crushed,_ or _their lives cut short_.

Some boys are simply experiencing the blues as captured in the piece below written by one of the Brother Authors.

2nd Grade Blues

by Thelonius Stokes

2nd grade blues . . .

Finger painting, in my world, I got the blues . . .

Just, struggling to ride my bike that I always use . . .

Today, after hearing the sudden ring of the ice cream

truck, I trip and fall . . .

Had to work out of my workbook today, couldn't even play

with my friends, I wish I could see them all . . .

Just got the brand new light-up, spider-man shoes, all I

was trying to do was show them off outside, scuffed

em up . . .

A day in school, and got a timeout, because I told my

teacher to shut up!

I went to lunch, and spilled my apple juice on the floor . . .

This girl ate all my cookies, and still wanted more . . .

I lost my show-and-tell toy . . .

I found out it was with this boy . . .

I went home, only to be in trouble with my dad . . .

He said, my teacher said I was just being bad . . .

I went to my room and stomped my feet . . .

It was so loud you could almost hear it from the street . . .

My sister went to go tattle tale . . .

I got yelled at again, I felt so pale . . .

I got the 2nd grade BLUES!!!!!

We simply enjoyed writing for young boys. Writing from a young boy's perspective, I attempted to capture a kid's aim for his future, one that he was looking forward to with anticipation of wonderful things. The boy was expressing his wants in the piece, *I Want to Be* . . .:

FEARLESS VOICES © 2013 by Alfred W. Tatum, Scholastic Teaching Resources

I WANT TO BE . . .

by Alfred W. Tatum

I want to be the fastest

I want to be the smartest

I want to be the strongest

I want to be the coolest

I want to be the richest

I want to be the happiest

I want to be the healthiest

I want to be the nicest

I want to be the sharpest

I want to be the neatest

I want to be the proudest

I want to be the worldliest

I want to be the awesome-est

I want to be the best person ever.

My seven-year-old son loved it. He added the line *I want to be the awesome-est.* I also wrote the following to capture kids' growing pains and pleasures.

Could Barely

by Alfred W. Tatum

I sat in the car.

I could barely see out of the window.

I went to the park.

I could barely shoot in the basket.

I went to the carnival.

I could barely reach the line.

I got a new bike.

I could barely turn the pedals.

I went shopping with my mom.

I could barely carry the bag.

I took a long trip.
I could barely stay awake.

I was racing my big sister.
I could barely keep pace.

I was playing baseball with my father.
I could barely throw the ball.

I watched a scary movie.
I could barely sleep.

I started doing things **made** for five-year-olds.
I could barely believe how much fun I was having.

My little sister came to my room.
She could barely do the things I do.

I could barely stop laughing.

Finding Their Roars as Young Lions

Within an hour, the boys became intentional in writing to build capacity. One young writer believed that young boys should find their roars as lions. He wanted to place this message in a piece for the very young among us who have yet to find their voices. His piece is below.

The Confused Lion

by Kristopher Kizer

There was this baby lion.
His name was Leo. Leo is a curious little cub. He was walking when suddenly he fell
    into a pond. Leo couldn't swim so he was just struggling to get out, but couldn't.
Then an army of cows comes along rushing through the grass. To come to Leo's rescue.
    They saw Leo. They welcomed him into the herd. Leo, of course, went with the herd.
The herd raised Leo as if he was a cow.
Leo did everything the herd of cows was doing. A couple of years went by and as Leo
    grew older he was still acting like a complete cow.
Eating grass and traveling with the herd of cows.

FEARLESS VOICES © 2013 by Alfred W. Tatum, Scholastic Teaching Resources

Until one day the herd was traveling deep into a forest.

It was a dangerous area.

Then, this big, fearless, and strong lion appears out of a tree and leaps on to these huge boulders.

Now the big scary lion was staring Leo and the herd in the face.

The herd of cows ran out of the forest because they were scared except for Leo.

Leo and the big lion just stared at each other.

They both didn't say anything. The big lion continued to stare at Leo. Suddenly, Leo felt fear and went running back to the herd.

The big lion watches Leo run and soon the big lion disappears into the forest.

The next day the herd of cows decided to head back to the forest.

As they walk, the big lion reappears.

The group of cows went running all the way back to where they came from again, but not Leo.

He stood in front of the big lion.

The big lion just ROARS at Benny!

Birds flew away.

Leo tries to roar. However, it sounded like a MOOOOO.

So the big lion ROARS again at Benny!

Leo tries to roar.

Again, a moo.

So the big lion ROARS again at Benny!

The big lion roars for the final time.

Leo roars even louder and strong then the big lion.

There was a great intense power in Leo's voice.

Leo now sounded like thirty overwhelming lions!

Leo cleared the whole area.

Animals were running all over the place.

His moo was now a roar.

The big lion stops roaring and glances at Leo.

The big lion says, "You are a lion now live like one."

The big lion disappears into the forest.

Soon Leo followed the big lion into the wild.

From that point Leo never acted like a cow again.

Leo followed the big lion to be what he always have been,
a lion.

Another writer placed a young boy on the superhero express. His piece is below.

The Superhero Express

by Noland Branch

I arrived at school bright and early today because dad didn't have to make my breakfast
today. I did it!

I ran to Suzy in art class.

"Suzy, guess what? Guess what? Guess what?"

Suzy cheered me on, "What! What! What Bray!"

"I was a superhero yesterday."

She was amazed. "Awesome! Wait a minute . . . For reeaalll?"

"I promise to Barnie."

"What was your name then?"

"The Pouncer, and I could jump how high and how far I wanted."

"Even to the moon!"

"Yeah, I went to New York. That's where my Big Bro Works."

"Then what?"

"Then I hopped to China. Bong! I took off. Bam! I landed."

"I ate a lot of rice there."

"Yummy!"

"Next! Next! Next!"

"I zoomed to Texas!"

"Whhoooaaah! My grammy lives there!"

"I walked around in a straw cowboy hat."

Suzy chuckled.

"Whoosh, I was gone. I screamed Wwweeeeeeee as I played tag with superman. I told him
look I'm just like you!"

"What did he say?"

"Good going kid."

"What happened next?"

"I woke up."

Other writers' words were more caustic and direct. The following piece is written by a
13-year-old who takes the stance of an older man.

FEARLESS VOICES © 2013 by Alfred W. Tatum, Scholastic Teaching Resources

Untitled

by Byron Mason

Kid, I see you growing and I wonder the direction.

Will the n**** in the world grip you in infection.

I wish to offer protection through my words throughout time.

But will you cut to the side or stand in the line.

The line being the accustomed and the side is the custom.

Wishing you more then I should and plus some.

Because influence is the woman and the product is the bosom

And you can choose to go below them or stay strong and above them.

And the world is scary and you may not see it but believe it because what an older man

Tells you, you should listen and receive it.

Some lead you astray but I would be a fool if I stood by in the line and let you become a tool.

Where you're going I'm not for knowing but the path I can show.

You've naturally grown in body, but it's up to you to grow in soul.

Breaking Bread as Young Intellectuals

Like so many writers before them, including the ones discussed throughout this text, the Brother Authors were breaking bread as young intellectuals in developmentally appropriate ways as they wrote for students a few years younger. They, however, still used the basis for writing for building capacity that can be identified across 300 years of African American male writing. Similar to their progenitors, the Brother Authors used the following as the basis for their writing:

1. Religion
2. Social conditions
3. Laws
4. Extant circumstances

Many of their writings were community-related and school-related, connected to their relationships with teachers and others within their personal circles. They became serious writers as they imagined the "ghost of the young brother" needing their words. They were not imprisoned by smallness by focusing on school-based metrics for writing such as rubrics. We wrestled with the following:

1. How can a piece of writing "live in the distance" because of its profundity?

2. How can one measure fearlessness in a piece of writing that refuses to be circumscribed by small ideas or ideas removed from the troubles of a people or the trouble of the world?

In the Key Point at the start of this chapter, I offered that writing carries a unique burden for the writer, his contemporaries, and future generations. I also offered that it requires a bit of courage, particularly if African American males are going to write with the intent to remove the "darkness" that circumscribes the lives of so many who look like them. Therefore, I end this chapter with a bellwether.

Spiritual Darkness

by Alfred W. Tatum

The salvation of young African American males

Has been sequestered by spiritual darkness

False Gods or bullet-induced fears

And cowardice by conductors on train tracks to nowhere

Seeking small solutions to save their own hides

Or, to at least pay the mortgage

Fear of persecution

Fear that persecution is not worth it

Because you dummies don't even know how to dress in the morning

How in the world will you then wear spiritual garments

You dress for Sabrina and Tina

To get you some

The best you can hope for right now

Because you have not found the divinity in you

It's not in the textbooks or classroom discussions

So you believe it's not worth it

Because the state did not authorize it for your teachers as part of their duties

This is your setting maul upside the head to keep you ignorant

So you can share nothing with your sons

Oops up your head

The living dead

I got you sucka

I turned out the lights

And you can't find the switch

But, you say it's better to smoke a blunt in the dark

Make unwanted babies

And sleep

I say find the light

Walk without fear

Tell God I am here

And stop trying to please false prophets

Stop being the world's sex toy.

This is your bellwether

A Critical Question to Consider When Supporting African American Males Writing to Build Capacity:

- Which authors' words do we continue to use to fully capture the African American male experience decades beyond their original copyright?

In the column below, I identified the characteristics of texts grounded in building capacity for African American males. Which texts can you identify that serve as exemplars of writing to build capacity?

Building Capacity	Identified Text
1. Teaching	1.
2. Providing guidance	2.
3. Becoming intentional	3.
4. Building agendas	4.
5. Providing an awakening	5.
6. Restoring the head	6.
7. Delivering a message to the people	7.
8. Laying a foundation	8.
9. Forecasting	9.

Clearly, what the government wants is not just death, but silence. A "correct" inmate is a silent one. One who speaks, writes, and exposes horror for what it is, is given a "misconduct."

—Mumia Abu-Jamal

CHAPTER 5

BE IT RESOLVED: VOICE AND VISION

In this chapter, I end with a discussion of the locus of African American adolescent male writers with the aim of shaping, promoting, and safeguarding their opportunities to write inside and outside of schools while teaching them to become excellent writers. More importantly, the goal is to teach them to move beyond silence. I have tried to excavate the locus of their writing for the past five years in relation to the four platforms that have been discussed in previous chapters only to discover that these young males are radically complex in their search for wholeness. They are struggling to find out what's at their core. I tried to get them to move toward their cores during the fifth annual Institute. I offered them the following poem on day 1 to set the tone for the writing:

KEY POINT

To write is to become familiar with your light and darkness and everything in between. It becomes the gray matter of your existence. Reading puts you in contact with others. Writing puts you in contact with yourself.

—Alfred W. Tatum

Calling All Jungle Brothers

by Alfred W. Tatum

Dark and light whispers

Hovering over ten-year-olds

Preyed on by the memories of older brothers

Who became their new art teachers

Black is the dominant color

It wipes out all other colors

It even wipes out Black in the Jungle

Where the rhythm of life

loses it beat

until the new drummers

wake up the sleeping giant

with sounds that rattle the earth

at its deepest core

where Blackness is the beginning, not the end.

I am a Jungle Brother in search of the core.

I then asked them the following questions:

1. What do you know about the author from the piece?
2. Which words make sense and which words need to be changed?
3. What questions or comments do you have for this author?
4. Do any of the lines stand out to you?

Identifying the Core

I wanted the young males to understand that there is a rhythm of life beyond each piece and that we were in search of that rhythm, whether real or imagined. The rhythm also has the potential to shake the earth at its core. It was this type of dialogue among writers that became the centripetal force. We were led by the words and an examination of the writer behind the words. The title, "Calling All Jungle Brothers," was pulled from my college days' radio listening experiences. The line, "hovering over ten-year-olds," captured a recent killing. "New drummers" refers to resilience while "waking up the sleeping giant" suggests capacity building. The starry-eyed youngsters had to wrestle with a cacophony of influences to pen their first piece of the new Institute. The dialogue and contexts were new. The freedom to write without

FEARLESS VOICES © 2013 by Alfred W. Tatum, Scholastic Teaching Resources

the stifling contours of a required topic or page length was a frightening prospect. Being summoned to look deep within their inner core—personal, cultural, community, gendered, developmental, aspirational, social, economic and academic—presented a new challenge. Many of the boys had become inmates to their own silence, unsure how to use their voices. This was the first barrier that needed to be shattered and excised. Getting them to examine a short piece quickly, "Calling All Jungle Brothers" in the example above, and writing immediately afterwards was the key. Two of the writers used the poem as their guide, drawing upon lines that stood out to them. One built on the idea of voice as sound (It's Time to Speak) and the other focused on the rhythm of life in Chicago (the lady in the red dress).

With Sound that Rattles the Earth

by Joseph Jordan-Johnson

It's Time to Speak
I have been shouted down, quieted by a harsh rebuke
Because one didn't think my words worthy of notice
Times where I've sheathed my tongue
Due to another being afraid of their prowess
It's never my intention to offend with my opinion
nor to raise an opposition to my belief
But there are times, there are chances when this may occur
And there, I will no longer keep my voice small and brief
I am an African American, and I indeed do have strong feelings,
But I express it not through fists, but words
And whether one thinks little or highly of me
I will ensure that my voice is heard
And when I do, it won't be just my words
For I hear them all
The angry whispers, heartbroken cries, informed thoughts
My ears extend and hear their call

Where the Rhythm of Life Loses Its Beat

by a Brother Author

We call her our lady in the red dress,
Flawless.
But, we allow bullet casings to cascade through her fingertips,
brass charring the webs of her fingers.

Feel Lake Michigan scratch against her legs,

Broken glass slicing her marble skin to crimson.

I want to save her.

But the shine on her brown irises has already faded.

I feel the chill ravage up my spine from within her stare.

We let the darkness consume her.

From this point forward, the Institute was on. The red writing sign that read "On Air" burned inside of us. We were becoming part of a long lineage of writers as we gave deference to ourselves. We had our own words to reflect upon and guide us. The African American male writers were guided by their own words; and their words, although grounded in different narratives and influences, became a projectile for more writing. The sooner they began writing, the sooner I was able to give individual feedback on word choice, spelling, punctuation, and content. I would assess the writing to determine the following:

1. If students' writings were trapped behind limited knowledge of a subject matter or narrow views on topics

2. If students were careless with facts, character development, or language use

3. If students' writing was stuck in the past without showing how writing about a particular topic had a modern-day resonance

4. If students' writing had an overreliance on what they already knew as compared to seeking out new information to give greater integrity to the writing

To illustrate the point, I recount a conversation with a young male who wanted to write about kidnapping.

TATUM: What are you writing about?

STUDENT: Kidnapping.

TATUM: What do you hope to accomplish with your writing?

STUDENT: Not sure.

TATUM: What do you know about kidnapping? Have you searched the Internet to get to the essence of kidnapping?

STUDENT: No.

I then directed the student to read an article about kidnappings that occurred in Mexico. We combined the terms and did a Google search. He discovered that reading about "real" kidnappings gave his story greater power. He also found a setting for his story. I also discovered something about the writer that I did not know or would not have known if I had not assisted with the search. His piece is on the next page.

FEARLESS VOICES © 2013 by Alfred W. Tatum, Scholastic Teaching Resources

Human Trafficking

by Armand Vasquez

I take another sip of the dirty water. Mom locked the blue, rundown door on me again, which is what she does every night. Cabron, leaving me on the streets. But that's OK because when I'm older, jo voy a America and will never come back to Mexico. Bad things happen on these streets. Guns blasting. I go in the trashcan for cover as I usually do. This is my life. Is this is my place, though? Tan loco, this can't be all there is, death and violence. This is not right. But here I am listening to bullets as a goddamn song. Then I hear the trash can open and a man tells me, "Get out, puto, you're coming with me." I cry. I scream. No one comes. No one hears. No one helps in my time of need. No one cares in Mexico. I'm alone, all alone. I refuse to go, but that's all I can remember when I was knocked out by the handle of a gun.

I wake up to eggs and ham, but I don't want food today. I'm in a small cell that is really uncomfortable, but I don't have a choice. Esto esta stupido. I ask the guards to take me home, but they don't. I call my mom but she doesn't come. I get tired and sleep, thinking of the worst that can happen. I scream, "Dios me ayude, ayudame." There's a window that I look through seeing the sun go down, orange, red, purple then black as night comes, until they come for me and put me in a room with a man. He's wearing a purple suit, white shirt and of course a purple tie. After awhile the big man began, "You can blame your mom for this BOY. She didn't pay me so I took you. The girls will love you, you're what they call . . . a pretty boy, OK kid."

"Who are you senor?" I ask.

"I'm your worst nightmare, kid, and your boss so I want you to have sex with the women we give and make their money worth it," he ordered.

"What is sex sir?" I question.

"You idiots didn't show him the movie, uhhh never mind give him to Chicara—she'll teach him everything."

We leave the room going to a bedroom, with a drunk women on it. "Lo guapo, I'm going to have fun tonight," she says.

"What do you want?" I ask.

"Quiero que esta noche," she said with a vile laugh.

"What should I do?" I asked. She told me things that I wish I didn't hear. She showed me what to do and I did. I did them to survive. I did it for my life. When done they put me in a grand cell with other boys.

"Hi there, I'm Pedro," a boy explained. "Hi. You like pineapple? I have some and I don't like it at all." "Jo gusto mucho and I have some apples I could trade you." That is what we did every day for days, weeks, months, and years.

Pedro became my best friend there. We lived there for ten years, made friends, then one day my friend Pedro and me made an escape, with food, two guns and a grenade. This is when things went wrong. Pedro was hit in the head with a bullet. This angered me to the worst measures. I put the AK-47 on my back, took the Desert Eagle from Pedro's death grip while I looked in his bright blue eyes and closed them myself. That day changed my life as I killed the men who put a gun to my head, who forced me to have sex with women who disgusted me, the men who laugh at me cry every night. How dare they. Joder them all. They're all dead. Every person involving my pain from this cursed place is dead. The boss, his men, all of them are now dead, 6 feet under. Now what do I do? Everyone is freed and they run while I watch them. But now what do I do. Pedro is buried. Now what do I do? I walk here and there. I eat now and then. I don't do nothing except wait for death to take me. Living life the best I can. I go to America tasting freedom on my lips. I smile on it all now with a good job, family, and friends. Now this is my story. This is my life. This is where I belong.

This young male, who had no idea what to write about, wrote a piece that brought the Institute to tears. This was our second day together. A day earlier, he wrote a piece about Michael Jackson in order to say he completed his writing for the day. This was unacceptable. He was reliving an in-school practice that demands students write for teachers. "Human Trafficking" was written to capture the feelings of kidnapped children trapped in a nation with little chance of being rescued. His use of Spanish entangled with English gave the story greater authenticity. It was the combination of research, questioning, and language use that gave his piece power. His confidence as a writer was stoked, and we all became more connected to a human tragedy because of his words. The four questions I used to evaluate the students' writings and discuss their writing with them led him to become a different writer. However, the young males still needed to develop their voices to share their powerful thoughts. They needed to move beyond their whispers.

Beyond Negotiated Whispers

One of the Brother Authors inspired the piece that follows, which focuses on finding collective voices to offset an enforced or accepted silencing. He wrote a piece and shared it in our writing space, but his voice was barely audible.

Negotiated Whispers

by Alfred W. Tatum

Silenced by an iron muzzle

Strapped to the back of our heads

Speaking with our eyes as our chests throbbed

Fourteen tongues tied together

Trying to negotiate a new language

The head bob said, "What's up, Brother?"

Our first whisper of rebellion

Strengthened as we learned to move beyond whispers

That had little chance to echo

Beyond the small space that consumed us.

The poem was inspired by knowledge of the iron muzzle fitted on the heads of enslaved persons who were accused of insubordination. In his autobiography, Olaudah Equiano, who wrote *The Interesting Narrative of the Life of Olaudah Equiano or Gustavus Vassa, The African* (1794), described his first encounter with such a device in the mid-1700s (see the image below).

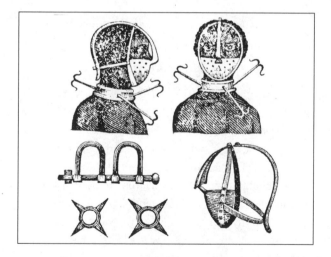

The young males read the poem in relationship to the image as they prepared to discuss ways to move beyond their individual whispers or shed light on the need to move beyond collective whispers.

Moving Beyond Collective Whispers
The Power Is Together
by Corey Ellis

I'm alone seeking help.

Wondering why so many days I see no one there with me.

I hear the calling but there is no light to fight the darkness.

Let us stand together.

Unaided I am weak but together there is no force that matches us.

Stand our ground and not let evil bring us done.

Break the chains, my fellow kin—you are not alone.

Make obvious show we are not clowns nor violent not what is shown on T.V.

NOW show them NOW, not tomorrow or next week.

In solitary the enemy has kept us and weak they've left us.

For the power is together.

Alone my voice is insignificant but side-by-side our voice is a MIGHTY ROAR heard to the
promised land.

The power is us—not one, but us, brother and all together at LAST.

Moving Beyond Individual Whispers
Strength
by Will Thorpe

My mother always said I was a survivor. There I was standing on the subway in the
heart of downtown Chicago. I was on the Jackson stop at the Red Line train. No matter
where I was I could never muster enough courage to feel like I had a sense of belonging.

I always felt this growing urge to die that constantly seeps in and runs its sharp fingernails
across my throat. I always planned the way I thought I should die. The methadone couldn't
finish me. My family thought I was a step away from creating a mass murder that would result
in my spirit being banished. In reality, I just wanted to end my existence.

The football players at my high school were the worst. When I went to school, they
beat me with stainless steel pipes and threw me in garbage cans. Have you ever got six
of your ribs broken and seven stitches in your eyelid?

As the train grew closer, I walked up towards the tracks. I could see my blood
splattered and my limbs ravaged. I could die in front of all these people and be
content. If I jumped in front of the oncoming train, would they finally notice me?

A short woman watching me said, "I was there too . . . Don't give up on life until life gives up on you." Without uttering a word—I showed her me. I showed her the stitches in my eyelid, the bruise marks from my cracked ribs above my waist, and the cigar burns my father mistakenly placed onto my skin. As I begin to pull the left sleeve up on my shirt to show her the rest, she stopped me.

She lit a cigarette and told me, "Listen kid, you're still beautiful no matter what . . . I've been in your shoes. I had my share of the cigar burns and bruises, but I made it through and I know in my heart you can too."

"You don't understand," I said. "Nobody could understand the way I feel." As she flicked her cigarette onto the train tracks, she walked closer to me and she hugged me. As I hugged her I realized that this is the closest I have ever been with another human. We hugged until the train moved swiftly passed the terminal. As the train passed, our mouths didn't emit sound but our bodies did. I could hear both of our hearts locking on to the same beat at the same rate. As my tears trickled down my face on to the hard pavement, she wiped my eyes.

Strikingly, both pieces written on the same day show the promise of community and the perils of individual pain left unchecked. "Strength" is a powerful piece of fiction that allowed us to feel the embrace of two strangers on a subway platform who were somehow connected. It gives permission to seek human contact when you feel silenced to live above a whisper that others may not hear. The other piece calls for a mighty roar. The instructional environment, the shared writings, and the context authorized a wide range of writings among African American male adolescents. The young males were empowered to:

1. Write to shed light on their own humanity
2. Write to increase understanding about socially significant phenomena
3. Write to create a pillar for new understandings
4. Write to move beyond their own silencing

They were also asked to write to tap into their lighter side, to simply bring joy and laughter. They wrote from a space where broad economic, racial, and social issues did not matter. They wrote children's stories.

At the Center of it All

Many young African American males get caught up in America's swaying winds inside and outside of schools. During the third day of the fifth Summer Institute, I heard a radio announcer mention, "The new KKK is Kids Killing Kids." I used this quote to remind the young writers what they were called to do:

- Be thoughtful!
- Be serious!
- Be unapologetic!
- Be fearless!
- Become part of the swaying winds!

The piece below, written by one of the Brother Authors, stands in stark contrast to "I Hope You" that captures a young male who is consumed by self-hate and misses out on a father-son bond. The author of "The Race" used a go-kart as a vehicle to show father-son bonding.

The Race

"Hey little Mac, did you come up with a blueprint of how the go-kart is going to look?"

"Not yet, Dad, but I'm working on what colors and wheels it's going to have."

"That's great, son, but we have to get to work with the actual go-kart. I'm going to pick up some wood from the store—I'll be back in half an hour."

While Dad was gone, little Mac bolted up the stairs, into his room, and quickly grabbed some colored pencils and paper from under his bed. First he wrote an outline of his go-kart on the paper with a regular number two pencil. He then filled it in with bright and vibrant colors, and to top it all off he added some flames on the side. When he heard the jingle of the door opening, he ran down stairs to show his dad the outline.

"That's great, son. I like every aspect about it. It's simple yet effective and creative."

Little Mac and his dad went out to the backyard to start working on their finished product. Dad cut the wood and pieced it together with a power drill. When the time came, little Mac painted it all by carefully, following the outline he had written for himself.

"Oh—I almost forgot the finishing touches," said little Mac.

He then went over to the back of the go-kart and painted "father-son bond" in real big letters. Dad looked at little Mac and smiled.

"Now it's ready," proclaimed Dad.

The day of the big race was exciting. Little Mac made sure to eat a breakfast of cereal and Dad had a cup of coffee. They got to the race area confident and humble as they prepared themselves for victory. Both Dad and little Mac strapped into the go-kart and put their helmets on. They looked around and saw all the other dads with their sons bracing themselves for the race.

"ON YOUR MARKS, GET SET, GO!"

As little Mac and Dad rode off into the sun all you could see was the "father-son bond" painted in big bold letters on the back of their go-kart.

Another author wrote about the joy and curiosity young African American boys have entering kindergarten. This was his counter-punch against the "at-risk" language used to describe young African American boys entering school for the first time. His piece is entitled "Spanky Kindergarten Mysteries":

Spanky Kindergarten Mysteries

by Jarell Charleston

I have a mystery this morning

Are we going to have fun in kindergarten?

I have another mystery this morning

Are we going to the zoo and see the lions in kindergarten?

Will we go to the park and play on the swings?

Will we play with the round ball in the gym?

Are we going to the swimming pool, the big one,

Like the one a shark can fit into?

Are we going to have dress up day

Like the one in the movie?

I have a mystery this afternoon

Will we go to the circus to see the lions, tigers, and bears?

When do we have lunch?

I have a mystery this afternoon

Do we have to go to sleep at school?

Are we going to have classroom parties

With lots of games, candy, and movies?

Are we going to read lots of books about cars, kings, and animals?

Will we learn our numbers from one to a thousand?

I already know mine—1 2 3 4 5 6 7 8 9 10, see—and much more

Will we learn our ABCs?

What if we know them already?

When do we get out of kindergarten class?

The teacher says,

I have a mystery, Spanky.
Can we finish with the first day of school
before we finish kindergarten?

This was simply a delightful piece aimed to remind us that Spanky is full of hope and possibilities, and that he will benefit by having others who respond to his youthful curiosity.

A Mosaic of Writers

The writers across five summers were fully engaged as they strove to change the narrative of who they are and how others should view them. They held a very balanced view of themselves. Reading and discussing the writings of African American male adolescents is like mapping the DNA of their existence. Their writings contain hope, serenity, and silliness. They also reveal pain, hard truths, and complexity. The range of their writings is captured in the chart below that emerged from an analysis of topics of the writings of year-five participants.

Topics/Frequency	Excerpts from the Brother Authors' Writings
Violence/Crime (15)	But, we allow bullet casings to cascade through her fingertips
Community/Street Life (13)	Yeah, I'm ignorant like that. I destroy my brain cells and spend half my day on the corner, Talkin' about the same things, Sayin' "Let me pull the trigger!"
Identity/ Self Questioning (13)	Am I the one deep in my shell or am I the one that is outgoing in life at all times? I got to know who I am in life. Am I the one that won't take life serious or the one that takes life as a joke? Am I the young Black boy that stands on the corner to work to make a living or am I just the Black boy that just wants to get by?
Education (11)	We went from discovering the secrets of the stars to only having money if we are a megastar. Do not look to be the next Obama, Bron Bron, or Oprah. Look to be better than them, better than anyone could have predicted. The sky is the limit. Education will skyrocket the brothers to the moon to educate your minds and reach a monk-like level of awareness.

Topics/Frequency	Excerpts from the Brother Authors' Writings
Inequality (11)	The truth is kept hidden by the dark cloak of anger, masked by the painstaking mistakes of ignorance. We are forced to lie down while we listen as society tells us a bedtime story about who we are and how we came to be. We are fed the expired box lunch of what the media has served, but that can no longer be healthy for us.
Racial Conflict (11)	The Stand Your Ground Law keeps you from getting harmed That covered a killing of an African American boy at 17. Was killed by a 9mm gun at close range though all he had was an Arizona fruit juice. All this did was enrage the Black culture. The lies and the violence have gotten people protesting. Blacks don't need to be uncertain. George Zimmerman is a man with no concern. That's why our brother Trayvon was only alive for a short time.
Resilience (10)	Fear my shadow dark skin and stare at weeded concrete when I walk by as I hold my head up high. I laugh out loud at racism and flip the bird at stereotypes. I am bulletproof, stainless steel.
Revolution (10)	I hear the calling but there is no light to fight the darkness. Let us stand together. Unaided I am weak but together there is no force that matches us. Stand our ground and not let evil bring us down. Break the chains, my fellow kin . . . you are not alone.
Drugs (7)	Emerging from the deep fog of fall my dark, compassionate, stern knight walks towards me. I pray that he has something to ease the pain. The pain of not knowing when my next meal is. I am nothing, but a pauper. So I count myself lucky for having him here. He has a companion with him: Ms. Edinburgh, the love of my life. This lad is lucky to be with this fair lady. My knight in shining armor runs toward me in zeal and yells: Aye, Poo, the dealers up on Lennox got the new testers. We need to hurry up before they run out of Oh, my knight in shining amour.
Perception (7)	They pierce me with eyes that could kill character and eradicate self-esteem. Monsters they call me. They don't know the person behind the Nikes. They only see what they want.
Despair (5)	Well, it's been two years since your death. We all have not forgotten what happened. The memory of you lying with that girl is stuck in my mind. I know that you were taken for no reason. But who is to blame for this?

Topics/Frequency	Excerpts from the Brother Authors' Writings
Mothers (5)	Before I could speak my mom came bursting through the door. She got up and presented saying, "I know it's bring your father day, but I am [his] father.
Slavery (5)	The Europeans forced us to dance to keep the mortality rate low as we sailed to the Caribbean. Stripped naked on their ships and forced our melanin to cry under the Atlantic sun. Have food shoved down our throats, and let the bile rot at our stomachs. Now we waltz along sea-side street corners, to ease the pain.
Fathers (3)	As little Mac and Dad rode off into the sun all you could see was the "father-son bond" painted in big bold letters on the back of their go-kart.
Love (3)	I thought nothing could ever take the place in my mind of your sweet angelic face.
Rebellion (3)	The government is brainwashing the youth. Why? So they can get more money for the taxes, as they say. Scared of the government because they have big guns; I have a Big mind that I'm not scared to fire.
Religion (3)	Gazing portals of heaven look upon and weep. Ole spiritual songs helped us. Ain't gonna let nobody turn me 'roun'. Wait until your change comes. Was it all just a "game"?
Sexual Exploitation (3)	In Dunbar Village, there is no law. No help to hear the villagers' call. The night air filled with terrors. Broken souls lamenting justice's errors, with mothers and girls being raped and put to shame.
Girls (2)	How could I, the skinny Indian kid, handle an Italian dame? The sweat dripped from my forehead as I boarded my train.
Peace (1)	In Life take what the world gives you. In Life live and love. In Life use the talent that God gave you. In Life remember that God saved you.

The topics are familiar, but the Brother Authors were instructed to write with a level of sophistication. Drugs became the knight in shining armor. Sexual exploitation was seated in a foreign village. Inequality became a dark cloak of anger. The freedom to anchor their writings in the four platforms yielded a counterbalance. Resilience became a companion to despair. Old Negro spirituals traveled alongside "Broken souls lamenting justice's errors." Slavery and rebellion became neighbors. At times, their writings were uniquely African American and male. At other times, there was a universality that had nothing to do with race or gender. The locus of their writing seems to be a need to achieve "voice," not a narrow voice, but one that captures the mosaic of their existence. Their voices give us a greater sense of their vision, but they also give us a greater vision of ourselves. This is why we must work to nurture the next generation of African American male writers.

Critical Questions to Consider for Becoming Writing Teachers of African American Males:

1. How can the writings of African American males be used as a professional development tool for teachers who are striving to shape and protect equitable pathways?

2. How do we ensure we are not foreclosing opportunities for African American males to display their full range of writings?

3. How do we use the writings of African American adolescent males to teach writing to younger African American boys in grades K–3?

4. How do we ensure that the voices of African American males are never muzzled in classrooms?

Educators cannot walk away from what it means to be human when engaging adolescents' multiple identities with reading and writing. They must experience their fullest selves during instruction.

—Alfred W. Tatum

PART 2

TURNING YOUR CLASSROOM INTO A LITERACY COLLABORATIVE

Reading and discussing substantive texts in an encouraging communal setting—our *literacy collaborative*—is one of the best ways to get adolescents involved in writing. This implementation section showcases the practical details—the instructional path, writing frames, strategies, mentor texts, questions, PowerPoints, and so forth—that I use to support young readers and writers, ages 11-17. While our work occurs across the five weeks of our Summer Literacy Institute, you can adapt the content and structure to meet the needs of your students and format, and work inside a writers workshop within a traditional English/language arts class or an after-school program, or you can create your own Literacy Institute. Regardless of your venue or format, the underlying principles and goals remain the same.

First, let's take a look at the overarching philosophy, theoretical stance, structure and content of AAAMSLI—then, we'll explore what this work might look like inside an English/language arts classroom.

Principles, Promises, and Platforms

All young adolescents struggle to define themselves as they work to make their way in the world. And all should have a sense of what they can do in the world to effect change for the better. Our literacy collaborative, the African American Adolescent Male Summer Literacy Institute (AAAMSLI), incorporates into its intellectual framework issues critical to the lives of adolescents and young adults—self-definition, resiliency, community, agency, social consciousness—and invites students to engage in critical inquiry and produce work within this broad approach to thinking and learning. If students struggle, we should first examine our own instruction; very often, the problem is not a struggling reader and writer but a student who lacks engagement in the materials he's being asked to read and write.

Few students—particularly those who are already suspicious of school—are going to spend their time with a text that doesn't speak to them. My work aims to address all students as strong thinkers who deserve access to the tools with which to frame ideas, formulate opinions, and address the big issues of our time. I surround my students with *enabling texts*, books or stories that are deeply significant and meaningful to young people. These are texts—authored by writers who represent a long line of people who themselves have overcome adversity—that form a *textual lineage* that speaks to the rich possibilities of a life both thoughtful and well lived. Enabling texts offer a road map to life for readers as each of them strives to develop an individual plan of action and a healthy psyche. Through the power of enabling texts, and the talk and writing they inspire, I aim to change the equation for teens—away from learned hopelessness, powerlessness, and grim acceptance of all the worst life has to offer and toward hope, resilience, productivity, and success. My work with these texts centers on *human development*, not simply reading and writing development. When working with teens who struggle with literacy, too often we give them *disabling texts*—books that, by my definition, focus only on skills and strategies and are often developmentally inappropriate. Such practices not only embarrass our teens but, in ways that prove destructive, undermine their self-confidence.

In AAAMSLI, we use transformational texts to provoke thinking, questioning, talking, and writing across the four platforms—defining self, nurturing resilience, engaging others, and building capacity. In this way, students start to listen to and value their own ideas as they put their voices on record and become fully engaged in their own literacy development.

GUIDING PRINCIPLES

AAAMSLI aims to strengthen the relationship of young readers and writers, our "Brother Authors," with literacy using the following guiding principles.

1. **We work with enabling texts.**

   We use texts that move beyond a sole cognitive focus—such as skill and strategy development—and encompass a social, cultural, political, spiritual, or economic focus. This contrasts with disabling texts, which reinforce a student's perception of being a struggling reader and writer. A disabling text also ignores students' local contexts and their desire as adolescents for self-definition.

2. **We regard writing as a mode of social action.**

   We find that different approaches for mediating writing helps these young men use raw writing to ask challenging questions, offer different perspectives, and get others involved in acting on issues affecting families, communities, countries, and the world. Language—reading, writing, speaking and listening—are interwoven and connected with action.

3. **We use the four platforms to recreate ourselves.**

   I want the Brother Authors to use their pens to change course, to conduct an autopsy of all things young, Black, and male. Our Institute is meant to give them the space and support to recreate themselves. They are charged to seek power and promise in their own words across the following four platforms:

   - **Defining self**

     Finding the language to put your voice on record without apology and without waiting for others to define you.

   - **Nurturing resilience**

     Remaining steadfast in the face of destabilizing conditions. Resilience can also be defined as having more protective factors than risk factors; factors that counterbalance risk encompass family as well as social, psychological, and behavioral characteristics that provide a buffer for youth.

   - **Engaging others**

     Engaging others is defined as bringing one's contemporaries into the fold to strive for a better humanity for all.

   - **Building capacity**

     Building capacity is defined as creating a foundation on which future generations can build their agendas.

   The four platforms provide progressively broader contexts for intellectual development, beginning with establishing individual identity and expanding to envisioning oneself as an active participant in society at large.

OUR GOALS

The goal is not simply to get the students to write, but to nurture a particular type of writing. The goal is to have them "write their lives" without compromise. To inspire them to that end, I post these lines of encouragement on the walls of our classroom for all to see—and then refer to them often. I'm convinced that surrounding the Brother Authors with bold and spirited words makes a difference and keeps them centered on our goals.

Why We Are Here

- To be courageous, bold, even heroic in our writing.
- To be part of a community of Brother Authors.
- To exercise literary freedom.
- To become urgent souls.
- To put our voice and vision on record.
- To become a student of humanity.

What We Aim to Achieve

1. Write to shed light on our own humanity.
2. Write to increase understanding about socially significant phenomena.
3. Write to create a pillar for new understandings.
4. Write to move beyond our own silencing.

FEARLESS VOICES © 2013 by Alfred W. Tatum, Scholastic Teaching Resources

WHAT WE WRITE

Each student writes a minimum of 30 pages of text over a five-week period and explores multiple genres—writing frames that help shape and structure their writing. Writing helps these students make sense of the complexity that affects their lives—their being, doing, and acting.

Poetic Broadside/Protest Poetry (at least three)

Poetic broadsides are short; they get right to the heart of the matter. And, as I explain in my book *Reading Their Lives: Rebuilding the Textual Lineages of African American Adolescent Lives* (2009), poetic broadsides typically share the following characteristics:

- They acknowledge pain/poverty fatigue.
- They are anchored by purpose.
- They are written out of necessity.
- They call for the next self-appointed leader—someone to build capacity among us.
- They ignite protest against self or others.
- The reject patience and waiting.

Black Shorts (at least two)

Blacks Shorts is a name I coined with my students to capture short stories that center on African American themes and experiences. Short stories, in general, are a terrific literary genre for teachers and students because:

- They often deal with a single event.
- They can be managed and paced more effectively in classrooms that include struggling, marginalized, and reluctant readers.
- They are great tools for modeling writing.
- They are a great means by which to wrestle with issues of social justice.
- They provide core experiences with a wide range of texts.
- They are authentic opportunities for teachers to write and share their writing with their students (Tatum, 2009).

Children's Story (at least one)

I also ask the Brother Authors to try their hand at a children's story, to explore their thinking and understandings for the next generation while they consider these questions:

- What do I say to young Black boys?
    - o What can I do/write to give young Black boys strength?
    - o What do I write to help young Black boys win any battle they may face?
    - o What do I write to a Black boy that focuses on his full humanity?

We pen children's stories for the next generation of young boys so that they smile, grow, laugh, and love as they make their trek toward their teen years and manhood.

First Three Chapters of a Novel

Taking on a novel—or at least the first three chapters—enables the Brother Authors to stretch themselves as writers. They are empowered to write to:

- Shed light on their own humanity.
- Increase understanding about socially significant phenomena.
- Create a pillar for new understandings.
- Move beyond their own silencing.

This writing is not created in a vacuum, of course; we read, mediate text, discuss, question, analyze and discuss and question some more. I share my raw writes; the students share theirs. Our immersion in text informed by our intellectual framework— the four platforms and key points—supports our thinking, writing, learning, and growth as human beings.

The Daily Schedule and Structure

Every day, I aim to have the Brother Authors writing within 30 minutes of each three-hour session, affording them more than two hours to write each time we meet. This daily agenda, with occasional variations (see Appendix B), frames our ongoing literacy collaborative. Note all suggested times in the following schedule are approximate.

Recitation of The Preamble (5 minutes)

The young males are required to recite the Institute's preamble to open and close each three-hour writing session. We also discuss its meaning at various points throughout the Institute; the authors gain new insights about its meaning as the days pass and they dig deeper into their writing. The preamble is meant to nurture a cooperative and conversational reading and writing community. In ways that echo the traditional African American involvement with text, we strive to create a communal approach.

Brother Author Warm-Ups With Explicit Instruction *(10 minutes)*

I then engage my students in a ten-minute focused target lesson in which I address an obvious instructional need that has appeared in the students' writing; this may range from instruction on conventions such as spelling and grammar to understanding the nature of voice and the essential need for well-organized writing (see Appendix C for samples).

PowerPoint Launch Plus First Raw Write and Critiques *(15 minutes)*

I launch our daily literacy collaborative with approximately six slides that feature provocative quotes and/or text excerpts. As I share the slides, I model my response by sharing my own reaction, engaging in a raw write—writing to live, writing for personal growth—and then encouraging my students to do the same. The key to getting the young males to write each year is to place my writing before them and open up my writing for critique.

Enabling Texts and Mediated Discussion *(throughout each session)*

Enabling texts play an essential role in our literacy collaborative. These are texts that matter for all students—texts that shape a positive life trajectory and provide a positive roadmap that can help students resist nonproductive behaviors (for recommended readings for diverse students see Appendix E). What's more, these are potent texts that naturally spark reading, writing, speaking, and action. I may read aloud from these texts to launch a discussion or engage in raw writing and ask the Brother Authors to do the same. I also assign the texts for homework.

We also welcome mentor authors into AAASMLI. Interacting with a successful published author has a tremendous impact on the Brother Authors. During our fifth Institute, we enjoyed a visit with Christopher Paul Curtis.

Writing *(1½–2 hours)*

Students write for approximately 1½ to 2 hours during each session and move initial raw writes, anchored to our four platforms, into powerful and polished writing around the four

Christopher Paul Curtis with two Brother Authors

required writing frames—poetic broadsides, short stories, children's stories, and the initial chapters of a novel. I circulate among the group conducting individual writing conferences as I see the need; Brother Authors may also request a conference.

Author's Chair or Voice Chair *(25 minutes)*

Every student has the opportunity to read aloud from his piece, one that's becoming—still in the drafting stage—as well as polished, final drafts. Getting real audience response is an indispensable part of understanding how a piece works and, if it doesn't, what can be done to improve and strengthen it.

Blog Posting

In our Institute, Brother Authors post their writing to our blog (see: http://aaamsli5.blogspot.com/blog). The goal is to reach an audience well beyond our own small group of fifteen Brother Authors.

THE WRITING ENVIRONMENT

In AAAMSLI, the Brother Authors work in a room at the University of Chicago that's filled with laptops and books, many penned and published by African American male authors. Bold posters and powerful quotes line the walls. The Brother Authors work at tables so they can easily collaborate and share their writing. The prevailing atmosphere is one of respectful urgency. Everyone is either reading or writing or discussing their reading and writing; it is for this reason that I often refer to our Institute as a literacy collaborative. One of the goals of our Literacy Institute is to create a communal approach to literacy that aligns with African Americans' historical relationship with literacy. Historically, reading and writing among African Americans were collaborative acts involving a wide range of texts that held social, economic, political, or spiritual significance (Tatum, 2009).

THE FIRST DAY AND THE PREAMBLE

On the first day of each Institute, I greet the young males with a handshake, a perssonal laptop computer that they can use for the duration of the Institute, and a copy of the Institute's preamble. I direct them to stand and read the preamble in unison with me, and I ask them to memorize it within 24 hours. On each subsequent day, then, we recite the preamble without looking at the printed text. I call on one or more of the young males to recite the preamble verbatim after we recite it as a group. I then ask them to explain its meaning. This is the opening and closing structure of the Institute and of each session.

The Preamble

We, the Brother Authors, will seek to use language to define who we are; become and nurture resilient beings; write for the benefit of others and ourselves; and use language prudently and unapologetically to mark our times and mark our lives. This, we agree to, with a steadfast commitment to the ideals of justice, compassion, and a better humanity for all.

To this end, we write!

POWERPOINT PRESENTATION ON AFRICAN AMERICAN MALE WRITERS

Since I'm working with African American male writers, I often share a Photographic Timeline of Black Male Writers to inform and inspire my young authors. I want them to know that they are joining an illustrious line of accomplished writers who have come before them. The Photographic Timeline features images of African American males across a wide range of disciplines whose writings are characteristic of the platforms discussed in this text. This is a representative sample of African American male writers past and present and does not represent an exhaustive list. I've enclosed my slides for you to use as well (see Appendix D). If you work with a different demographic, by all means, search for authors who will speak directly to your own students. Most diverse students haven't had access to the stories of and texts created by diverse writers; this is your opportunity to change that.

Now, what do you do if you don't have the luxury of a three-hour daily writing period with your students? Are the goals that guide my work in AAAMSLI still possible for you to implement? Absolutely. You'll need to adapt in ways that work best for you and your students. Rather than thinking of my schedule as a daily template, regard it as an instructional menu from which you choose each week, using every supportive component—the PowerPoints, enabling texts, the focus lessons, and so on—but alternating them across the days and weeks.

THE ESSENTIAL LITERACY CONTENT AND UNDERSTANDINGS

Let's examine the heart of the literacy content and understandings around which I build the four platforms and our literacy collaborative:

- Enabling Texts
- Raw Writing
- Writing Journals
- Teacher as Writer

Again, when students are immersed in enabling texts and raw writing, they aren't simply engaged in advancing their reading and writing skills and proficiency. Rather, they are exploring, analyzing, and questioning the social, cultural, political, spiritual, and economic forces that define our lives, and, as a result, students are drawn into speaking and listening, reading and writing. And for those working with the Common Core, implementing a dynamic integration of the language arts is a key charge.

Enabling Text

Your role in helping students understand how to mediate and analyze text is essential. Draw on the conceptual framework of the four platforms and the key points I suggest as well as the questions you and your students generate as you read, write, and discuss. Demonstrate the stance and language of literary analysis. What does it look like and sound like to engage in an analytical discussion about a book, fiction or nonfiction? What language do you use? How do you draw on evidence from the book to support your position? Students will learn as you prompt, model, and mediate, not only through book study, but also throughout the day as you create a rich analytical literacy collaborative.

MENTOR TEXTS

The best way to support young writers is to provide them with multiple models from other authors—and, ideally, from you as well. Writing and sharing your writing with your students is uniquely powerful. The goal, of course, is to spark their own writing in response.

Many teens lose interest in reading and writing—often at the point in their lives when these activities became more about schoolwork than storytelling. The only way to invite students back to literacy is to reformulate our approach to and presentation of what they view as the culprit—literature itself. My work, then, centers on reframing writing as shared self-expression, using short, powerful biographies and mentor texts from authors with varied backgrounds—African American, Native American, Hispanic-American, Asian-American, soldiers, rap artists, ex-prisoners, established poets, social activists, teens, and more (see Appendix E). I believe that exposing students to a broad and flexible range of writing gives rise to a breadth of thinking and fosters openness.

Guidelines for Discussing Mentor Texts

- Share your observations briefly; the goal is to get your students to discuss.

- Prompt your students to share their own thinking and observations about the mentor text.

- Encourage them to refer to specific passages or ideas that most affected them, or to jot down quotes that struck them as particularly powerful.

- Call attention to word choice: how do these specific words contribute to the overall effect?

- Ask students to pay attention to the voice and style of the writer; how does the writer get across ideas to the reader?

- What kind of mood does the author create?

- How does the writer convey action or create tension?

- Encourage analysis and critique to help students demystify the writing process as much as possible.

- Remind the students to use the "assessment language" that they are learning from you (see pp. 133–134) as they discuss and evaluate the mentor text.

Mediated Book Discussion

Pivotal to forming collaborative communities around literacy are these two guideposts:

1. Exhibiting caring.
2. Reflecting before rejecting.

In practice, the behaviors that stem from the guideposts and enable productive discussions include the following:

- Speak firmly but kindly.
- Express caring even though you may be upset or angry.
- Practice honesty in all communication.
- Use reason instead of pulling rank.
- Apologize later if you say something you wish you hadn't said.

Learning to disagree without being disagreeable is the goal. Help your students learn such phrases as, "I am not sure I understand you correctly," or "I have a somewhat different interpretation," or "This is how I see things."

Raw Writing

One of the best ways to engage teens in literacy is to invite them to create their own texts. Writing offers students a new kind of power as they craft—through their own writing—a stronger sense of self. And then, as they figure out their own visions and voices through their personal writing, they may well find a way into texts written by other authors. The National Commission on Writing (2006) makes clear the transformative power of writing:

> *If students are to make knowledge their own, they must struggle with the details, wrestle with the facts, and rework raw information and dimly understood concepts into language they can communicate to someone else. In short, if students are to learn, they must write.*

You'll find raw writing, the honest and unapologetic "voices on record," an indispensable tool in your work with your students. You'll see that the power of raw writing extends well beyond your classroom as your students emerge newly empowered to ask society challenging questions, offer different perspectives, and get others involved in acting on issues affecting families, communities, countries, and the world.

Again, like enabling texts, raw writing is not about practicing strategies or skills; it's about helping teens use writing unapologetically to explore their place in the world. The critical importance of this experience is perhaps best summed up by these poignant words, penned by one of the young AAAMSLI participants:

> *"You can take my life and my mind too. You don't have to take my heart; I'm giving it to you. But the one thing you will never get is my pen because without it I'm nothing. Writing is the only thing I have left." (Tatum, 2010, p. 90)*

Remember that raw writing is meant to be free form; a means of recording unedited thoughts, of establishing one's voice as a writer. Raw writing is a means of representing, recording, recounting, and reflecting as it acquaints students with time and space, appeals to both individuals and groups, and encourages writing for oneself and others.

MULTIPLE STANCES

And as soon as your students have something on paper, you'll want to begin a process of reviewing, critiquing, and questioning to help them dig back into their writing to see it again and think about what their next steps might be to strengthen it. You might consider following my lead: I circulate among the boys and pull a chair up alongside them when I spot a teachable moment or when they signal they need a conference. In general, we want our teen authors to assume three different stances as they use reading and writing to:

- **Respond as writers.**
  Students write in response to the PowerPoint launch, the enabling mentor texts, and our enriching classroom discussions.

- **Analyze and critique.**
  Students reflect and comment on writings by mentor authors, peers, and themselves.

- **Write as readers.**
  Students refine writing to create polished pieces that they can share with an audience beyond the classroom.

Writing Journals

In AAAMSLI, we have access to laptops for every Brother Author. I recognize that few classrooms have the same benefit; if computers are available, typically they are housed in a computer lab and students must sign up to use them. Given this reality, I recommend that you encourage your students to keep a writing journal. In general, the writing journal serves as a lifeline to text and the conversation about the text that you and your students enjoy through your daily classroom conversations. Through their writing, your students develop an intellectual and emotional bond with each text they read; the journal also helps them organize their thinking and become more analytical as they can revisit their thinking and extend and refine their original ideas. Writing captures their thinking and makes it visible so they can return to it and revise it with new insights and questions.

Here's a quick rundown of the various ways in which your students might use their journals.

POWERPOINT LAUNCH

During the PowerPoint launch your students can capture the points you make or new insights that come to them about the platform, key point, and additional themes and ideas that are in play in your classroom each day. The journal is an important keeper of big ideas, new insights, and questions for inquiry at another time. It's also the best place to keep their raw writes and all attempts to extend and develop their raw writing into polished poetic broadsides, short stories, and beyond.

INDEPENDENT READING AND RAW WRITING

The writing journal may become your students' best companion during the solo work of independent reading. In the journal they can capture their questions, predictions about what might happen next, intriguing facts they want to remember, notes to themselves about additional research they may want to do as a follow-up to their reading, reminders of topics they want to explore in writing—in sum, the journal is a way to capture the rich, ongoing conversation that takes place in the head of every reader as he or she engages with the world the author has created on the pages of a book. The writing journal can serve the following functions:

Notekeeper: They can keep track of their peers' ideas, comments, and questions about the text under discussion. Their notes also work as place-holders and memory joggers—so they can jump into the conversation and recall precisely what they wanted to share. They also then have a record of the conversation that ensued that they can consult and use to shape the raw writing they may choose to do after they've read an enabling text.

Personal record of growth: Your students will enjoy keeping track of the range of ideas and topics they covered in their book study groups; over time, they can see how their thinking has deepened, their engagement with texts become more meaningful and analytical. The writing journal becomes a helpful keeper of their personal relationship with books and their developing journey as readers and writers who understand how to use both to define self, nurture resilience, engage others, and build capacity.

Source of Assessment Information: Writing journals offer one of the best ways for you to keep track of and monitor your students' evolving understanding. The journals are an invaluable source of information about the nature of your students' thinking, the level of their participation and contemplation, their ability to change their thinking as new evidence appears, and so forth. And for your students, the advantages of writing extend across the book study—before, during, and after.

Teacher as Writer

Students benefit from teachers who write with them. These teachers serve not only as models but they are also better prepared to help students "get their voice on record." When you have grappled with choosing a topic, or searching for language that matches your feelings and ideas, you can more easily provide concrete, constructive suggestions to student writers facing similar challenges.

SETTING THE TONE

As you lay the foundation for a strong writing community, you may wonder how to help students feel comfortable writing, especially about what truly matters to them—often a tightly guarded secret. In these early sessions, support any writing that seems to come from their lives, no matter how undeveloped or unpolished in form. The aim is first for students to gain access to themselves—to use writing as a means of discovering the power of their own ideas, responses, feelings, and voices.

Putting It All Together: How It Unfolds in the Classroom

Let's zero in on how this might go in your classroom; let's say you have a 60-minute class period, plus or minus; the period might unfold something like this:

WRITING WARM-UPS AND EXPLICIT INSTRUCTION

Again, as I implement in AAAMSLI, you might want to devote approximately ten minutes to explicit instruction, focusing on the specific skills and strategies you note your students need to keep developing as proficient readers and writers. Typically, skill instruction is most effective when it addresses skills your students demonstrate they need.

FEARLESS VOICES © 2013 by Alfred W. Tatum, Scholastic Teaching Resources

THE LAUNCH: POWERPOINT PRESENTATION

I show an average of six slides that address an essential question or key point. The PowerPoints provide an emotionally and intellectually challenging kickoff for the broader inquiry, which plunges students into real-world issues encapsulated by the key points. The PowerPoint presentation is like a tutorial, meant to stimulate reaction and discussion as well as give students information they can use in their text discussions and raw writing. The PowerPoints may include controversial content, but their primary purpose is to expand on an issue, present a range of viewpoints, and get students motivated, engaged, and smarter about topics of social, even global, consequence.

The PowerPoint also sparks the first raw writing in response to what is seen and discussed. I create an open and encouraging tone for each writing session. Our writing atmosphere is nonjudgmental and dynamic, prompting the young writers to take to their laptops or writing journals without apology.

ENABLING TEXT AND VOCABULARY STUDY

The PowerPoint launch may be followed by a short, substantive, thematically linked selection that relates to a key point that you might read aloud to the whole group. Each selection serves as a mentor text for the inquiry. The reading leads to inquiry-based discussion and pushes forward together toward understanding. And again, students—and you—engage in a raw write in response.

Vocabulary Study

As part of this mix, I also always introduce at least three new vocabulary words, often words that relate to *academic vocabulary*. Isabel Beck's work is useful to this discussion. She divides vocabulary into three tiers: Tier 1 refers to frequent, everyday words; Tier 2 are those powerfully useful words that enable us to succeed academically; and Tier 3 words are *domain specific*, related to specific content disciplines, words like *amoeba* or *photosynthesis* (obviously, tied to biology). Help your students consider the *force of choice*: why did you choose this particular word and what impact does it have on your thinking and writing?

Reading and Writing Deeper

Once students have seen the PowerPoint presentation and engaged in raw writing, they are ready to go deeper, which may mean circling back to one of their earlier pieces and working on it to ready it for public sharing with the whole group and beyond (through the group blog).

Remember that you play a critical role as a member of the classroom writing community. Be open about your own writing strategy with students. Initiate a discussion by mentioning where you like to sit and whether you habitually write at the computer or prefer to use pen and paper. Where appropriate, share examples of your writing at various stages from raw to refined, remain open to critique, and encourage students to assess their own and each other's work with similar openness.

THE AUTHOR'S CHAIR

Every student must have the opportunity to share his work in the Author's Chair. In this way, your students share their new writing lineage—providing background and information on their inspirations and influences, and presenting the writing they have created—as well as providing and receiving the critical feedback that helps them evolve as writers.

- I typically introduce the Author's Chair by sharing one of my own pieces and encouraging the students to critique my work. I talk about how I might revise my writing based on my students' feedback.
- Then I challenge the students to share and refine a piece of their own. Again, I set the tone by warmly greeting each author as he takes the chair, leading the feedback and assessment conversation.
- The author's peers listen carefully, appreciate the work, and provide feedback on its strengths first, before identifying one aspect that could benefit from further development.

Suggestions for the Student Writer Who Is Sharing

- If you chose to write a memoir, talk about how you developed your memoir, why you chose specific memories, and how you approached the task. If you chose to write about something else, discuss your inspiration for that topic and format.
- Identify specific areas of your writing that you want your peers to focus on with the idea you'll refine at a later date.

Suggestions for Listeners

- Listen for ways in which the writer's particular voice makes the writing unique.
- Observe the way that details in the piece relate to the writer's central message.

FEARLESS VOICES © 2013 by Alfred W. Tatum, Scholastic Teaching Resources

The Questions That Guide Our Writing

We focus on the merits of the writing; of each piece we write we ask:

Vision and Voice

- Does it linger in the mind after it is read?
- Did the writer take care with his messages and his words?
- Is its attention to language fierce or lukewarm?
- Is the first sentence "perfect"?
- Is this writing worth reading outside of the Institute?
- Does it have universal appeal—even outside the Institute?
- Is the writing a *back-pocket piece* that other people world want to read again and again or pass on to others?

Craft

- What do you know about the author of the piece?
- Which words make sense and which words need to be changed?
- Is there evidence that the writer knows the conventions and mechanics of writing?
- What questions or comments do you have for this author?
- Do any of the lines stand out to you?
- Does it have any superfluous parts or is it "fat-free"?

ASSESSMENT

In my Institutes, assessment is primarily a tool for communication, used to help writers develop their voices and approach writing analytically to deepen their understanding of the craft. Sharing work and critically evaluating one's own work as well as the work of others are integral to our writing experience. Thus, my approach to assessment reflects the conversational community of our classroom. I examine writing within a sociocultural frame; I encourage my student writers to consider their audience beyond the classroom and to listen hard to the work of others. Student engagement in assessment is essential. I aim to help students identify their voice and then to establish a relationship with the reader. The African American male writers are guided by their own words; and their words, although grounded in different narratives and influences, become a spark for more writing. The sooner they begin writing, the sooner I'm able to provide individual feedback on word choice, spelling, punctuation, and content. I ask myself these questions as I assess the writing to determine the following:

1. Is the student's writing trapped behind limited knowledge of a subject matter or narrow views on topics?

2. Is the student careless with facts, character development, or language use?

3. Is the student's writing stuck in the past without showing how writing about a particular topic has a modern-day resonance?

4. Does the student's writing lean too heavily on what he already knows as compared to seeking out new information to give greater integrity to the writing?

5. Is the student struggling with conventions?

   - spelling
   - grammar and sentence structure
   - punctuation
   - paragraphing

Professional Development

Many African American males in school have not yet hit their stride as readers and writers, in part because of the narrow literacy instruction they encounter that fails to address their depth of need. Their failure also stems from the limited literacy instruction authorized by district administrators and principals, who tend to focus on minimum standards or simply meeting national norms, the low-hanging fruit of literacy reform efforts. In the process, educators fail to consider the broader contexts that inform these students' lives. This is why I have called for a more comprehensive model of literacy instruction for African American males in grades K-12 that brings attention to curriculum orientations, roles of literacy instruction, and the ways to teach text to nurture reading, writing, and human development (Tatum, 2012; Tatum & Gue, 2010, 2012). We should not focus on one while neglecting the others.

Becoming Writing Teachers of African American Males: Critical Questions to Consider

1. How can the writings of African American males be used as a professional development tool for teachers who are striving to shape and protect equitable pathways?

2. How do we ensure we are not foreclosing opportunities for African American males to display their full range of writings?

3. How do we use the writings of African American adolescent males to teach writing to younger African American boys in grades K–3?

4. How do we ensure that the voices of African American males are never muzzled in classrooms?

A Note About the Common Core State Standards

We must place the Common Core State Standards (CCSS) in the larger reform narrative, examining both the promises and potential shortcomings. Many large-scale reforms have failed, yielded lukewarm success, or dissipated. Still, I am cautiously optimistic as one who favors the CCSS. However, I want to offer two points: (1) the absence of sanctioned standards is not the root cause of the reading and writing outcomes for African American males, and (2) the implementation of the Common Core State Standards will not be at the epicenter of African American male academic success.

The Common Core State Standards are merely a proposed lever for addressing the uneven academic performance of students and addressing the dissatisfaction that state governors expressed about the academic preparedness of graduating high school seniors entering the workplace or colleges. We need Common Core Plus (+). Teachers who figure this out will place themselves well ahead of the curve while others are focusing on key staples of CCSS—close reading, complex text, and the balance between fiction and nonfiction–components that fit neatly into a checklist and can be assessed. The CCSS represent a point on a continuum; they are not the endpoint of the continuum for African American males. However, the CCSS align well with the historical pathway taken to advance the literacy development of African American males (see the table).

Conceptual Framing for Literacy and African American Males

Historical Orientations of Literacy for African American Males	Orientation of the Common Core State Standards	*Agreement
Reading and writing, debating, critiquing, and being able to make meaning of one's identity. Securing freedom and becoming self-determined. Establishing platforms to secure civil, economic, educational, political, and social rights. Building agendas to improve and enhance the condition of the African American community.	Providing appropriate benchmarks for all students, regardless of where they live. Defining the knowledge and skills students should have within their K-12 education careers so that they will graduate high school able to succeed in entry-level, credit-bearing academic college courses and in workforce training programs. Including rigorous content and application of knowledge through high-order skills. Preparing students to succeed in our global economy and society. Increasing complexity in what students must be able to read so that all students are ready for the demands of college- and career-level reading no later than the end of high school. Requiring the progressive development of reading comprehension so that students advancing through the grades are able to gain more from whatever they read. Ensuring that teachers across disciplines focusing on reading and writing to build knowledge within their subject areas.	Low

Curriculum and Texts

Historical Orientations	CCSS	Agreement
Reading texts that included classics from English writers, laws of the land, national and international news, letters, sermons, speeches, poetry, narratives, essays, biographies, broadsides, and short stories. Literature, science, humanities, and history texts were all prominent as reading across multiple subject areas was a common practice.	Reading a diverse array of classic and contemporary literature as well as challenging informational texts in a range of subjects to broaden their perspectives. Mandating certain critical types of content for all students, including classic myths and stories from around the world, foundational U.S. documents, seminal works of American literature, and the writings of Shakespeare. Focusing on complex texts outside of literature to ensure that these standards are helping African American males to prepare to read, write, and research across the curriculum, including history and science.	High

Writing

Historical Orientations	CCSS	Agreement
Producing texts that defined their lives and defined their times.	Writing logical arguments based on substantive claims, sound reasoning, and relevant evidence.	Moderate to High

Language

Historical Orientations	CCSS	Agreement
Using language to (re)claim the authority over them and counter oppressive and harsh circumstances (Tatum, 2009). Sharing knowledge, promoting ideas and cultivating a scholarly and literate way of life (Belt-Beyan, 2004). Cultivating speakers and thinkers.	Growing their vocabularies through a mix of conversations, direct instruction, and reading. Expanding students' repertoire of words and phrases. Preparing students for real-life experience at college and in 21st century careers. Using formal English in their writing and speaking and making skillful choices among the many ways to express themselves through language. Gaining, evaluating, and presenting increasingly complex information, ideas, and evidence through listening and speaking as well as through media. Having academic discussions and being able to deliver formal presentations in a variety of contexts. Collaborating to answer questions, build understanding, and solve problems.	Moderate to High

* Low = 0 to 1 connections; Moderate = 2 to 3 connections; High = 3 or more connections

A close look at the chart reveals a synergy between the historical orientations of literacy development for African American males and the emerging CCSS. There is more similarity with curriculum and texts, writing, speaking and listening, and language. With regard to curriculum and texts, there is a call for a wide range of texts. Writing has been central to the advancement of African American males. However, there is a radical difference between the conceptual frames and literacy in African American males (Tatum, 2013).

BOOK REFERENCES

Anson, R. S. (1987). *Best intentions: The education and killing of Edmund Perry.* New York: Vintage.

Baldwin, J. (1963). *The fire next time.* New York: Random House.

Christenson, L. (2000). *Reading, writing, and rising up: Teaching about social justice and the power of the written word.* Milwaukee, WI: Rethinking Schools.

Cose, E. (2002). *The envy of the world: On being a Black man in America.* New York: Washington Square Press.

Davis, C., and Walden, D. (Eds.). (1970). *On being black: Writings by Afro-Americans from Frederick Douglass to the present.* Greenwich, CT: Fawcett Publications.

Dunbar, A. M. (Ed.). (2000). *Masterpieces of Negro eloquence, 1818–1913.* Mineola, NY: Dover.

Gregory, D. (1964). *Nigger.* New York: Pocket Books.

Hinks, P. P. (1997). *To awaken my afflicted brethren: David Walker and the problem of antebellum slave resistance.* University Park, PA: Penn State Press.

Hodges, G. (2010). *David Ruggles: A radical Black abolitionist and the underground railroad in New York City.* Chapel Hill, NC: The University of North Carolina Press.

Hornblum, A. M. (1998). *Acres of skin: Human experiments at Holmesburg Prison.* New York: Routledge.

Kennedy, R. (2003). *Nigger: The strange career of a troublesome word.* New York: Pantheon.

McCall, N. (1994). *Makes me wanna holler: A young Black man in America.* New York: Vintage.

Mullane, D. (1993). *Crossing the danger water: Three hundred years of African American writing.* New York: Anchor.

Parks, G. (1970). *Born Black: A personal report on the decade of black revolt 1960-1970.* Philadelphia: J. B. Lippincott.

Porter, D. (1995). *Early Negro writing, 1760–1837.* Baltimore, MD: Black Classic Press.

Shelby, T. (2005). *We who are dark.* Cambridge, MA: The Belknap Press of Harvard University Press.

Singer, J. (2006). *Stirring up justice: Writing and reading to change the world*. Portsmouth, NH: Heinemann.

Tate, W. F. (2008). "Geography of opportunity": Poverty, place, and educational outcomes. *Educational Researcher, 37*, 397–411.

Tatum, A. W. (2013). Common Core State Standards: Structuring and protecting equitable pathways for African American boys. In. S. Neuman & L. Gambrell (Eds.), *Reading instruction in the age of Common Core State Standards.* Newark: DE: International Reading Association, pp. 75–89.

Tatum, A. W. (2009). *Reading for their life: (Re)building the textual lineages of African American adolescent males.* Portsmouth, NH: Heinemann.

Thomas, K. (1990). A different brand of education: Programs trying to reclaim a generation of black youths. *Chicago Tribune*, October 14, 1990.

Story Matrix

Focus on Middle and Secondary Schools

Facts about African American Adolescent Males	Myths about African American Adolescent Males	African American Adolescent Males and Education	*Chatham North Lawndale Bronzeville West Pullman Garfield Park

* Neighborhoods in Chicago

Add sources here:

Research and Prep Chart

Facts	Title	Sentence(s)	Name/Place

Rubric

Brother Author _____ Date _____

Self-Regulation/Evaluation	Peer rating 1
ORGANIZATION: The events follow a logical sequence.	4 3 2 1 0
INTEREST LEVEL/MOMENTUM: The story is interesting and keeps the reader involved.	4 3 2 1 0
SITUATED: The story is clearly situated in a time and place.	4 3 2 1 0
AUTHENTICITY: The story seems real and believable.	4 3 2 1 0
CARE: The author took care to provide the necessary details.	4 3 2 1 0
WORD CHOICE: The author chose words that capture the reader, and words that seem to fit.	4 3 2 1 0
VOICE: The voice seems real and authentic.	4 3 2 1 0
TOTAL:	

Additional comments to the Brother Author:

Daily Agenda: Five Samples

This daily agenda frames each writing session:

1. Brother Author Warm-Ups—approximately 15 min.
2. Explicit instruction—approximately 10 min.
3. Students writing for approximately 1 to 2 hours during each session (this includes time for research).
4. Sharing and posting to the blog—approximately 25 min.

SAMPLE 1

- Brother Author Warm-Up
- Voice chair—student reads his work in front of peers to receive feedback.
- Explicit instruction: Planning as a writer
- Guidelines for the day
- Writing
- Sharing and posting to the blog

SAMPLE 2

- Introduction to spelling and grammar tool on the computer
- Posting poems on the blogs
- Print out one of yesterday's poems to use in the voice chair
- Brother Author Warm-Up
- Voice chair
- Explicit instruction: Developing a "plan to write" matrix
- Writing
- Sharing and posting to the blog

SAMPLE 3

- Brother Author Warm-up
- Reading the first paragraphs of short stories: "The Pocketbook Game," "Thank you, Ma'am: Almos' a Man," "Marijuana and a Pistol," "The Almost White Boy"
- Explicit instruction: Writing the first paragraph of a short story
- Daily guidelines
- Writing
- Sharing and posting to the blog

SAMPLE 4

- Discussion
- What are you willing to sacrifice to save your Brother? Your life?
- How can you stop somebody in his or her tracks with your writing?
- Make me listen to you without telling me I have to listen to you.
- Brother Author Warm-Up
- Read "Lefty" with a short story rubric.
- Reading Short Stories: "Thank you, Ma'am"/"Almos' a Man"
- Explicit instruction
- Voice Chair

SAMPLE 5

- Making me listen to you without telling me I have to listen to you.
- !!!!!! and ALL CAPS—are these ever necessary?
- Brother Author Warm-Up
- Read "Two Feet" with a rubric.
- Finish short stories and print them out.
- Voice Chair
- Distribute
  - Read this book as a writer over the weekend. Finish it.
  - What makes this a classic?
  - Make notes about what the writer is doing.
  - Look at page 1, page 7, and page 9.

Writing Warm-Ups: Four Samples

Brother Author Warm-Ups are used to focus students' writing or research. They are also used to provide feedback to student writers. Students' writings or the instructor's writings from the previous session are selected for the warm-ups.

SAMPLE 1

Brother Author Warm-Up

IMPROVING THE VOICE AND WORD CHOICE

What is voice? Written words that carry the sense that someone—a unique human being—has actually written them.

There are bombs standing

there are bombs standing
on the corners of the cities
waiting to explode
at the slightest touch
baggy shadow street boys
stand cocked ready to fire
their eyes are grenades

they are warriors looking for a rite of passage
they are young lions

What feedback regarding voice and word choice might you offer this writer?

What additional advice might you offer?

Clogged

outside the black gate

where I once roamed

is the image that haunts me

an image that I hate

the green grass absorbs the death of a 30-year-old

the dirt becomes soiled again with blood dripping from his chest

my two-year-old nephew

asks about the sleeping man

he lays on the ground to imitate the corpse

surrounded by the police tape

I am struck by his innocent depiction of death

he remains motionless

before the cop yells to get him out of the crime scene

He weeps when hearing the thunderous voice

I weep too for my nephew and the thirty-year-old

connected for that brief moment by their poses

One breathing, the other breathless

I grab my nephew's hand and walk him away from death

hoping the image quickly fades away

the image that continues to haunt me

clogging my . . .

everything

the devil didn't even anticipate this

He's ready to retire

before the summer starts

His most profitable season

What feedback regarding voice and word choice might you offer the writer?

What additional advice might you offer?

AFRICAN AMERICAN MALE FACT FINDER

Add one fact about African American males

1. _____

   Source of information _____

2. What are two myths people have about African American male adolescents?

   • Myth 1:

   _____

   _____

   _____

   • Myth 2:

   _____

   _____

   _____

Brother Author Warm-Up

SENTENCE COMBINING

- His writing was original. His work met with opposition from critics of the time.
- Improving the voice and word choice
- What is voice? Written words that carry with them the sense that someone has actually written them.

Running

Police sirens start,

As fast as I could,

Down the alley,

Over the gate,

Shine in my eyes,

Hands behind my head,

Face on the cold brick wall,

In the squad car I go,

BUT IT WAS ALL HIS FAULT . . . .

What feedback regarding voice and word choice might you offer the writer?

What additional advice might you offer?

What do you think you know about the author from his writing?

Silence!!!

The world has many eyes and ears out there
And if you knew that, you wouldn't be sitting here
    right now,
In my face, explaining yourself
Sure you talk, explain yourself
But who will ACTUALLY want to listen to you?
After all, you have lied to us all . . .

Silence!!!
The truth will set you free,
But in your case, the truth will bring nothing but
    devastation—Hurt,
Have you thought about all the lives you have
    messed up, or have ruined because of the
    mistake you have made
The MISTAKE you have caused?
The only option for you is to MAN UP, and take full
    responsibility,
But that chance is over, there is nothing that you
    can do . . .

Silence!!!
Is everything . . .

There is no need to explain yourself
We can see right through you
Can see your pain, can see your fears, can see
    YOU
Now that we know the real you, we can torture
    you
Destroy you, the way you destroyed us
You didn't think of no one but yourself
And by you doing that, no one wanted to talk
    to you

Silence!!!
You don't have a friend
I'm not a friend,
He, she, it, and or they are not your friend
How can you be a friend unto us,
When you don't have a heart
When you say something
It comes out of one ear, and exits out
    the other.

Silence!!!

Writing Tidbit:

Quotation marks are visual clues to show readers when dialogue is used in a written work. Notice that the comma is placed before the end quotation mark.

"I'm going to offer you something more valuable than money," he said. "I'll give you a chance to learn to write."

—From *Black Boy*
  by Richard Wright

What feedback regarding voice and word choice might you offer the writer?

What additional advice might you offer?

What do you think you know about the author from his writing?

Brother Author Warm-Up

PLATFORMS

1. Defining self
2. Becoming resilient
3. Engaging others
4. Building capacity

Writer's Quote:

"I will be as harsh as truth, and uncompromising as justice . . . I am earnest, I will not equivocate, I will not excuse, I will not retreat a single inch, and I will be heard."

Danger

From a former Olympic champion to the president of food,
While a Mexican politician is assassinated by fools
The longest serving senator is gone at 92.
Not a lot of people know this and yet it's all in the news.
Left.
I mean if I could slam down the mallet of death
The juries ballots can't make the arrest.
The judge is stringed
Puppeteer fiends on the cover of news magazines
Government?
A 16-year-old male black Republican
I'm elephant tusk
The demo isn't tusker then us
They're mere mortals
And I've entered the portal to revolution.
I see the lies and executed 85 on the night of the long knives
Swastika in my eyes
But I'm a popular guy says the blueprint. Right.
Who knows the disease,
Or how a massive explosion can blow up 80 million trees?
Say cheese, smile for the camera.
It's the American thing to do.
Craft a smile out of a vile twisted malicious pursuit, of money.
You've lived the drama, tagged with a hulk swagg

Incredible ain't it? The green made us famous.
Now we styling with rich rags.
Custom made shoes but I walk no better
No further, no farther, no purpose so why bother?
And we could just do it, but I'll stay with the X
They call it a swoosh but I'm looking at checks
The freedom of speech is censored.
Life was never simple.
Ancient underground geniuses giving thumbs up with a thimble
And to cover it up the money that's under us.
Such a religious nation, in God we trust.
The suburbs be hell bent when they tear down the projects
The eagle just feeds on people using excuses like "progress"
Evolution is a process and this is not the first step.
Black people are not niggers.
Check the dictionary, it means ignorant does it not?
Man, knowledge is scary; it's like ancestors in a plot.
Not really observed like contracts that curve words
But secret assassinations and set-ups are hard bargains.
That's why I handle corporations with a
Long sword and armor
And my shield never yields to dogmas
Everything is questionable.
Dangerous, aren't I?

Safety is peace

Safety is something to share

Safety is rare

Safety is not everywhere

Safety is where you can't be afraid

Safety is always in the shade

Safety is nothing to be ashamed

Safety is know as no danger

Safety is always good during the weather

Safety can be no injuries

Safety is a place with harmony

Safety is the action of keeping safe

Safety is home or a place

Safety is important

Safety has to be supported

Safety is good

Safety should be in the hood

Safety brings faith

Safety can come in all different shapes

Underline one or two lines from the Brother Authors' writing samples that capture your attention.

Which platform(s) of social justice do you see emanating from these writing samples?

Questions for the BAs:

Let's talk.

Brother Author Warm-Up

SOCIAL JUSTICE

- Refers to the concept of a society in which justice (truth) is achieved in every aspect of society.

  - o   Individual and groups receive fair treatment.

  - o   There is a fair share of benefits in society.

  - o   Advantages and disadvantages are distributed fairly.

    1. Schooling

    2. Housing

    3. Neighborhood quality

    4. Economics and job market

    5. Legal system

    6. Entertainment

    7. Humanity

- Platforms:

  1. Defining self

  2. Becoming resilient

  3. Engaging others

  4. Building capacity

Writer's Quote:

"I will be as harsh as truth, and uncompromising as justice . . . I am in earnest, I will not equivocate, I will not excuse, I will not retreat a single inch, and I will be heard."

—*William Lloyd Garrison*
Editor, The Liberator

Writing Sample

To begin with, the number one pressing issue for young men is gang violence. I say gang violence because when you don't have anyone to talk to or you don't have any friends, you look to gangs because gangs are always together and are always taking up for each other. When you join a gang, they consider you family and they treat you like family, but joining a gang only leads to jail or death and you'll be all by yourself just like you started.

The second issue is drugs. I say drugs because most men these days are using drugs. One of the reasons is peer pressure; everyone starts using drugs and if you're not, they start making fun of you. Then, when you get tired of people laughing at you, you start using drugs. Then, before you know it, you're hooked on drugs and you just can't stop; then you wish you had never given in.

The last reason is finding a job. It's hard for most black males to get a job and I say it's hard because most males aren't able to get a job—because of the two reasons I listed in this essay. If you're involved with a gang, most likely you're going to go to jail, and with that on your record no one will want to hire you. And if you're addicted to drugs, it will show in your appearance and you'll be a hazard in your work environment. In conclusion, these are the issues pressing young black men today.

How can this Brother Author capture these ideas in a short story?

Underline two phrases from this Brother Author's writing sample that could be used as a title.

What platform or social justice issue do you see emanating from this writing sample?

- Platform _____

- Social Justice Issue _____

Close your eyes for 25 seconds and think about details of your neighborhood. Jot down five details.

1. _____

_____

2. _____

_____

3. _____

_____

4. _____

_____

5. _____

_____

Writing Tidbit:

Think about the following questions as a writer:

1. What topics interest you?

2. What allows your own voice to be heard?

3. What makes your writing easy?

Bring On the Day!

Wake up, wake up, it's a new day
Preparing for the trials that come my way
Fiery darts I dodge so precisely aimed
Like drug abuse, hot girls, and gangs
It's easy to get distracted after being taught
    to paper chase
Trying to get some amazing grace
But it's hard to get favor 'cause of the
    complexion of my face

And on top of that most of us are the head
    of the house
Although we're too young to have a spouse

Forced quick to become a man
But never taught to hold on to God's
    unchanging hand
Yet here I stand
With success and failure in each hand
Will I falter in my ways letting time go by
    like sand
But I tell myself, NO! With the thunderous
    voice only black man can
You see now I'm old enough to understand
That everything is possible with the right
    tools in your hand
So go head! Charge on! Because here I stand

(continued on next page)

(continued)

Come forth try to do the worst you can
'Cause the war doesn't always go to the
    strongest man, but also to the one
    who can withstand

I'm ready! With more than just a fighting
    chance
Suited and booted in my fighting stance
You knocked me down once; it's not
    gone be that easy again
And it's no secret you won't be
    victorious in the end
SO BRING ON THE DAY!!

What feedback regarding voice and word choice might you offer the writer?

What additional advice might you offer?

What do you think you know about the author from his writing?

Writing Sample

I could see the steady stream of traffic below my window. But, I never asked where the traffic was going until yesterday after the notice came. It was the same notice my friend, Butchy, received. He is gone now. It was always rumored that the bricks would come tumbling down. The stories behind the bricks will always be there, but the old brown bricks will soon be replaced with the new, more expensive bricks. The closets behind the new bricks will be larger, and the faces behind the bricks will look much different. I asked my mother, "Are we coming back after the new bricks are up?" She just said, "I don't want to live here anymore. It won't be the same." Deep down inside I knew that she would have trouble affording the new bricks on her salaries. There was a beautiful sign down the block that read—New Homes starting at $475,000. I like the pictures on the sign, but that's a lot of money. I guess it costs a lot of money to replace a boy's memory.

What feedback regarding voice and word choice might you offer the writer?

What additional advice might you offer?

What do you think you know about the author from his writing?

NEIGHBORHOOD FACT FINDER

Add one historical fact about your neighborhood

1. _____

    Source of information _____

2. What are two myths people have about African American neighborhoods?

    • Myth 1:

    _____

    _____

    • Myth 2:

    _____

    _____

Writing Tidbit 1:

Quotation marks are visual clues to show readers when dialogue is used in a written work. Notice that the comma is placed before the end quotation mark.

"I'm going to offer you something more valuable than money," he said. "I'll give you a chance to learn to write."
—From Black Boy by Richard Wright

Writing Tidbit 2:

A comma is placed before and after a person's name. See the example below:
    It was the same notice my friend, Butchy, received.

Photographic Timeline of Black Male Writers

Jupiter Hammon
1711–1806?, Poet

Venture Smith
1729–1805, Biographer

Olaudah Equiano
1745–1797, Biographer

Absalom Jones
1746–1818, Abolitionist & Clergyman

Richard Allen
1760–1831, Educator & Writer

James Forten
1766–1842, Businessman

Peter Williams Jr.
1780–1840, Episcopal Priest

Samuel Cornish
1795–1858, Journalist & Publisher

David Walker
1796–1830, Anti-slavery Activist

Theodore S. Wright
1797–1847, Author & Speaker

John Russwurm
1799–1851, Journalist & Editor

William Whipper
1804–1876, Abolitionist & Businessman

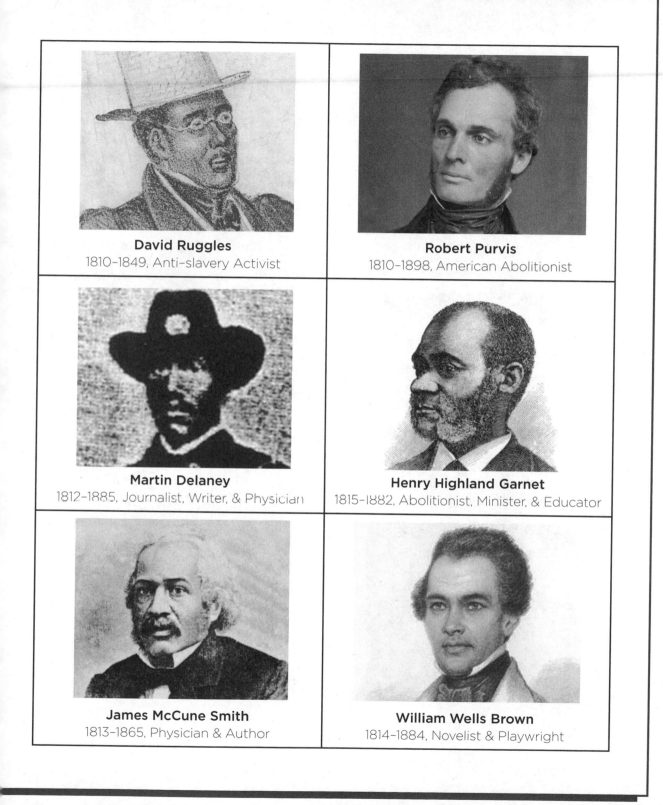

David Ruggles
1810–1849, Anti-slavery Activist

Robert Purvis
1810–1898, American Abolitionist

Martin Delaney
1812–1885, Journalist, Writer, & Physician

Henry Highland Garnet
1815–1882, Abolitionist, Minister, & Educator

James McCune Smith
1813–1865, Physician & Author

William Wells Brown
1814–1884, Novelist & Playwright

William C. Nell
1816–1874, Historian & Journalist

Samuel Ringgold Ward
1817–1866, Newspaper editor

Frederick Douglass
1818–1865, Writer & Activist

Alexander Crummell
1819–1898, Scholar

Booker T. Washington
1856–1915, American Educator

Paul Laurence Dunbar
1872–1906, Poet, Novelist, & Playwright

Charles Chesnutt
1858–1932, Essayist

W.E.B. Du Bois
1868–1963, Scholar & Sociologist

Alain Locke
1885–1954, Writer & Philosopher

James Weldon Johnson
1871–1938, Poet, Journalist, Critic

Claude McKay
1889–1948, Writer & Poet

Charles S. Johnson
1893–1956, Sociologist

Jean Toomer
1894–1967, Poet & Novelist

Rudolph Fisher, 1897–1934
Novelist, Short Story Writer, Dramatist

Sterling Brown
1901–1989, Poet, Folklorist, & Literary Critic

Arna Bontemps
1902–1973, Poet

Langston Hughes
1902–1967, Poet, Novelist, & Playwright

Countee Cullen
1903–1946, Poet

Richard Wright
1908–1960, Novelist, Short Story Writer, Poet

Robert Hayden
1913–1980, Poet, Essayist, & Educator

Ralph Ellison
1914–1994, Novelist, Critic, & Writer

James Baldwin
1924–1987, Novelist, Essayist, Playwright, Poet

LeRoi Jones/Amiri Baraka
1934– , Poet & Writer

Elridge Cleaver
1935–1998, Writer & Political Activist

Walter Dean Myers, 1937– , Novelist &
Poet, Children's and Young Adult Author

John Edgar Wideman
1941– , Writer & Professor

Don Lee/Haki Madhubuti
1942– , Author & Poet

Ellis Cose
1951– , Journalist, Author, & Editor

Walter Mosley
1952– , Novelist

Christopher Paul Curtis
1953– , Children's Author

Nathan McCall
1955– , Author

Percival Everett
1956– , Writer & Professor

Michael Eric Dyson
1958– , Author & Professor

John McWhorter
1965– , Linguist & Political Commentator

Kevin Powell
1966– , Poet, Writer, & Political Activist

Aaron McGruder
1974– , Cartoonist

12 Sources that Capture the Wide Range of Writings of African American Males

Armstrong, W. (1969). *Sounder*. New York: HarperTrophy.

Baldwin, J. (1985). *The price of the ticket*. New York: St. Martin's Press.

Dunbar, A.M. (Ed.). (2000). *Masterpieces of Negro Elegance: 1818-1913*. Mineola, NY: Dover.

Ellis, C., and Smith, S.D. (2005). *Say it plain: A Century of African American speeches*. New York: The New Press.

Everett, P. (2001). *Erasure*. New York: Hyperion.

Hooper, L. (2007). *Art of Work: The art and life of Haki R. Madhubuti*. Chicago, IL: Third World Press.

Hughes, L. (Ed.) (1967). *The best short stories by Black writers: 1899-1967*. New York: Little, Brown and Company.

McWhorter, J. (2000). *Losing the race: Self-sabotage in Black America*. New York: Perennial.

Mullane, D. (Ed.). (1993). *Crossing the danger water: Three hundred years of African American writing*. New York: Random House.

Porter, D. (1995). *Early Negro writing: 1760-1837*. Baltimore, MD: Black Classic Press.

Roessel, D., & Rampersand, A. (Eds.) (1994). *Langston Hughes: Poetry for young people*. New York: Sterling Publishing Company.

Thomas, C. (2007). *My grandfather's son: A memoir*. New York: HarperPerennial.

USEFUL WRITING RESOURCES

Dillard, A. (1989). *The writing life.* New York: HarperPerennial.

Truss, L. (2003). *Eats, shoots & leaves: The zero tolerance approach to punctuation*. New York: Gotham.

Zinsser, W. (2001). *On writing well: The classic guide to writing nonfiction*. New York: Quill.

Letters to Future Brother Authors

The Brother Authors are required to write a letter to the future participants. These letters capture their experiences and the benefits they garner from writing together.

Greetings, Dear Future Brother Author,

I write this letter to you because I learned so much from this program, and I want you to get the same lessons the program passed on to me—and more, if you can. I came into this lesson only partially educated about black writing, and I wrote solely for the benefit of a good grade. Here, however, I was able to write from the depths of my heart, from the brother I held down there because I didn't want to write words that would offend others, that would speak my mind without a care as to the feelings of my audience. Coming here released me from those bonds, it showed me that I was free to tell the world how I felt. I didn't need an MLA format or rubrics to tell me what I should write; instead, I received a pencil and paper (actually, a laptop) and faced a wide horizon, with my first step facing anywhere I wanted it to go.

At first, it feels weird, to just write what you feel. When I came here, I thought that Mr. Tatum either actually was going to restrict our writing was just throwing money at us, and that we'd learn nothing from this program.

I'm utterly glad that I'd seen that my thoughts about the program were completely wrong.

What I learned from here, what I am now able to carry along with me for the remainder of my life, is much more than I could have ever hoped to learn from a single place. Like you, I learned to just write whatever comes to mind, and to share my thoughts with fellow Brother Authors. It actually felt pretty good to share my thoughts with others, since I'm usually reserved and feel that others would render my thoughts towards my own culture as unimportant. Being in the midst of other young black males has not only encouraged me to share these thoughts about my race, but to take in what they had to say about us and to see how their voices come out in their writings, which was a fantastic experience.

By now, you would have written at least 14 different works. I truly hope that you have poured your soul into your writings, as I have done for mine. Now that we are Brother Authors, writers who are striving to make a change "for the benefit of others and ourselves," I will be looking forward to reading your excellent pieces on the blog. I know Mr. Tatum has done a fine job of tasking you with several objectives, and I have one last task for you as you set out after this program is over: keep your warrior intact with your soul. Don't ever take it out because someone may have felt offended by your writing. Keep true to what you feel, and stay proud in knowing who you are. That's the lesson we're setting out for other brothers, for those who have a voice and those whose lips are forever silenced. Keep this in mind as you walk out that door, and I promise you that your life will never be the same.

With best hopes,
Brother Author #7

Dear Future Brother Author,

I write this letter to you because I want you to have the same experience I had in this Institute. It was great to let my words of feeling flow on paper. I also got a few things off my chest that I wouldn't tell anybody too. I came to this Institute expecting to sit down and write anything on my mind, but there are different areas where you have to let your writing take over to poems, short stories, children's stories, and three chapters of a story of your choice. You will expect to write for the benefit of others and yourself. You will also use your language, which is English, prudently and unapologetically, marking our time and lives from slavery days to MLK and Obama becoming president. You will learn to not hold back on your own writing about anything.

You will remember your ancestors and keep them alive in the present. So, if you are reading this short letter, just know that you will like coming to this Institute to write about your feelings and whatever else you have on your mind. Dr. Tatum is a good guide to help you find something you can't think of at any moment. I can just say it's easy to trust him. —BA#6

Dear Future Brother Authors,

I write this letter to you because I want you to understand that you should always educate yourself. The mind is a terrible thing to waste and so is your youth! You should never waste time worrying about trivial issues! You are a writer! Go out and save people! You have so much power with your pen! Writers have the power to incite emotions, to convince, to empower, and to create webs of details that have the minds of others wandering! You have power within your pen!

When I came to this Institute I never expected to gain so much knowledge. As a writer, the knowledge I have gained has become precious jewels that I will always treasure. In school, I never really learned that you should always become more intelligent after you write. Before the Institute I only wrote about things I knew about. My writing never expanded. After the Institute I can honestly say that my writing has expanded drastically! You can expect to grow as a person and as a writer through this Institute. At the beginning of the Institute you may feel like you are lost as a writer, but at the end of this Institute, I assure that you will find your voice.

When writing, you should always think outside of the box. You should never feel like you have limits.

Write to save yourself and identify who you are. The pen is a deadly weapon; use it with caution.

Dear Future Brother Author,

I write this letter to you because I want you to know that you shouldn't be afraid of what you write. It's time people heard your voice and saw what you're capable of. There is something tamed inside of you that wants to come out, so let it out. Much more can be accomplished with a pen and paper. Wars were ended by the stroke of a pen. Why not show what you can start? This Institute is the place for a reserved writer to become an "Author."

From White Shoe Willie, to Juice Johnson, or a knight in shining armor—anything is possible. Who will you make next to pique the minds of others? I came into this Institute thinking it was all smoke and mirrors with no way of showing me how to hone my skills. But it turned out to be a wonderful experience with lessons I never knew. The people you'll meet are one of a kind, and the opinions are much needed. Trust me, it helps me improve drastically.

You will learn how to become the voice others need. You will learn things certain schools don't teach and come to know what a real "Brother Author" is. You aren't just given the title—you earn it, so show Dr. Tatum and the world how to speak "prudently and unapologetically." I loved this program and how it brings young brothers together, I'll use what I learned here to teach the minds of everyone I know, and you should do the same. —BA#2

Dear Future Brother Authors

I write this letter to you because I want you to understand what a beautiful opportunity you have to write in this program. In this program, your writing will soar to new heights, your writing will go to a place where it's never gone before.

I came to the Institute expecting another boring program that my mom signed me up for.

You can expect a fun, challenging program where you meet other Brother Authors and learn new things about writing different kinds of pieces like short stories, children's stories, poems, and more.

You will learn how to use language in an unapologetic way where you use your writing to touch others and engage others.

Have fun and write to benefit others as well as yourself. If your writing can make a father reconsider leaving his children or prevent a teen pregnancy, then your writing has helped others.

Your Brother Author

Dear Future Brother Author,

I am writing this for you because I am trying to bring the best out of you. You're the next generation of powerful black men that can lead their communities. You have the power to change your city for the best because there is nothing we cannot do. I am positive that the world will recognize you, and you have to go out and get that recognition. The only way people will know that you exist is to tell them, and the best way to tell them is to write. I can tell you that the Institute will be fun. There are a lot of great people around you, and you will want to stay here forever. Nevertheless, the Institute is only for 5 weeks. I hope that you will realize your full potential because it is there. The capacity to change yourself comes from within. Always believe that you can actually change the world, and you will go far.

Sincerely, BA#5

Dear Future Brother Author,

I write this letter to you because I want to help you realize that you are far more powerful than you think you are. The power of a writer

that lurks inside you is waiting to explode; be seen, heard, read, and felt! I came to the Institute expecting to just be writing and writing, and write some more. I was right! Moreover, my writing was critiqued by fellow Brother Authors, and their insights on my writing helped me develop the skills I needed to make my writing more powerful and realistic. You can expect not only to improve your skills as a writer, but also to develop a bond with your fellow Brother Authors—one that will hopefully last a lifetime. You will learn how to live the Preamble through your writing, by expanding your knowledge on certain topics and widening your imagination.

Quote from RB

"Let your words shape your future."
From last summer's BA#4

Dear Future Brother Author

I'm writing this letter to raise the sprit that is within you. You have a great deal of authority within the hands that follow power, peace, joy, pain, and happiness. I want to tell you to be prepared to write when you walk through the doors of the Reading Clinic. Don't be afraid to walk through the fire with your writing.

I came to this Institute expecting to learn how to write better than I already knew how to. I was also expecting just to write with a lot of boys who wanted to be writers. I was expecting to set my soul free through my writing. I was expecting just to write about black people and their struggles in life.

Expect to live with your eyes open at all time of the day. Expect to learn the preamble because it is the yellow brick road in which we walk, talk, and write. Expect to write.

You should learn the voice inside of the cage that wants to be released. Learn how to define yourself in many different ways in your writing. You will learn how to engage others with your writing; encourage the reader so they know that they can make it through the storm.

Remember that there is a writer in all of us. We can change the world with one pen at a time. Talitha Cumi Damsel Arise means rise up and be you. —BA#14

Dear Future Brother Author,

I write this letter to you because I want you to ignite the power available at your fingertips. You have the greatest responsibility to empower the generations to come with your knowledge, experience, and efforts through your pen. It's daunting, but the reward that comes with your talent is so much greater. Writers learn to warp their words to help and inspire others, and you will do the same. As a returning brother author, I came back expecting to improve on what I had learned from the first time at the Institute. Through what I learned from my time away, I practiced shaping my craft into something to be shared with my colleagues and the children that would come after me. I had the privilege to have my writings critiqued and be pushed for publishing by Dr. Tatum, and I will be forever grateful for being given the opportunity to have my writing shared among hundreds of people. You can expect to write—everyday. You will learn not only to write from a personal, creative space, but a universal one. People will look to your writing and be able to connect from their own experiences. You will be responsible for the inspiration of your posterity, and use that. Shape the minds of people who are lost in the world, let them know that someone is writing out there for them and their feelings. There are people who need a book, something to hold in their hands that contains so much knowledge and a spore of information. Writers shouldn't be afraid to share their stories. Being afraid of it means that you have something to lose. You put something into your story that you want to be heard, and made yourself vulnerable in the process. Use those nerves to your advantage. It is time for you to understand the power you have been given and use it. Make yourself vulnerable, because information is easier to convey through emotions rather than rhetoric.

Brother Author 10, 2012

Dear Future Brother Author,

I write this letter to you because I want you to understand that your writing can make a change to this society, help others, and define who you are to the world. When I came to this Institute I was expecting to be pushed and taught new ways to write. I will take this new learning to high school so I can exceed to the highest level I can. You will learn how to write in your comfort zones and your uncomfortable zones. I had a great time and a great experience here at this Institute.

From, BA#15

Dear Future Brother Author,

I write this letter to you to because I want to explain what goes down here in AAAMSLI. I came to this Institute expecting that we would just . . . write, but it was more to it than that. You see, I had to learn that I couldn't write from just experience, but from research. Dr. Tatum, your brilliant teacher, told me I needed to teach and learn when I write. Not only does it teach, but it also makes writing more powerful. You can expect to make many revisions to make writing sweet and for you to be strong. You'll learn what a pen can do and, trust me, it's much stronger than a sword. Write Hard! BA#12

Dear Future Bro Authors,

You will learn a lot from Tatum so take as much as you can.

He will help you with your trouble
And he'll tell you all he can.
Make him your friend and you will not regret it.
Brother Author 11—AV

INDEX